VICTOR BEWLEY'S MEMOIRS

Fiona Murdoch

VERITAS

First published 2002 by
Veritas Publications
7/8 Lower Abbey Street
Dublin 1
Ireland
Email publications@veritas.ie
Website www.veritas.ie

ISBN 1 85390 687 5

A catalogue record for this book is available from the British Library.

Cover design by Pierce Design
Printed in the Republic of Ireland by Betaprint Ltd, Dublin

*Veritas books are printed on paper made from the wood pulp of managed
forests. For every tree felled, at least one tree is planted, thereby renewing
natural resources.*

CONTENTS

ACKNOWLEDGEMENTS

Many people were instrumental in helping to bring about this book. I am particularly grateful to various members of the Bewley clan who, over the past few months, have grown accustomed to receiving phone calls from me at all times of day and night. I am most especially indebted to Victor's three daughters, Winifred Murdoch, Rachel Bewley-Bateman and Heather Bewley, his sister, Doris Johnson, and his sister-in-law, Mary Bewley. Also, his nephews, Patrick Bewley, John Poynton, Richard Bewley and Roger Johnson, and his niece, Margaret Warnock.

Many people outside the family also helped with the process of cross-checking information. In this regard I wish to thank Lena Duff (Victor's loyal secretary for many years), Monsignor Thomas Fehily, Annie Dunne, Bernard O'Gorman, Peter Lamb, Glynn Douglas, Valerie O'Brien, Ian Broad and David Poole.

I am also indebted to Gráinne O'Toole of the Irish Traveller Movement and the staff of the *Irish Times* Library, The Gorry Gallery, The REHAB Group and Government Information Services. Among those who made my task easier with their advice and encouragement were my father, Brian Murdoch, Joan Johnson, Rob Goodbody, Rev. Patrick Comerford and Ivan O'Brien.

Thanks are due, too, to those who joined in the hunt for photographs. As well as family members, a number of Campbell Bewley Group employees joined in the search – namely, Veronica Campbell, Mary Treacy and Catherine Toolin.

I wish to express my thanks, too, to the Veritas staff who have helped the dream become a reality. I am especially grateful to Maura Hyland, Toner Quinn and Amanda Conlon-McKenna.

And last, but certainly not least, I wish to thank my six-year-old son, Ruari, for putting up with a rather preoccupied Mummy over the last few months!

FOREWORD

'What's it like, having a famous grandad?' I was often asked at school. The first couple of times children posed this question I just looked at them blankly before replying that they had made a mistake: my grandad was not famous. I mean, I knew that Victor Bewley was in charge of Bewley's Cafes, and I'd seen his picture in the papers from time to time. I'd also heard him on the radio and TV talking about Travellers. But that didn't mean he was famous, did it? To me, he was just 'Grandad'.

Over time, however, I submitted to peer pressure and decided that I must have got it wrong – my grandfather must be famous after all. And so, at the next family get-together, I sidled up to him and asked, 'Grandad, what is it like being famous?'

He gave one of his gentle chuckles before saying, 'What on earth makes you think I'm famous?' That was a good enough answer for me. If Grandad didn't think he was famous, then he couldn't possibly be. After all, he should know.

★ ★ ★

During my teenage years I came to understand that my grandfather refused to see people as famous, or otherwise. He believed that everyone was of equal worth and that everyone should therefore be treated with equal respect.

Nevertheless, in researching this book I have discovered again and again the high esteem in which people hold him. Every phone call I made to someone outside the family produced the same response: as soon as I mentioned the name, Victor Bewley, people launched into warm tributes to him.

I've lost count of the number of times I have heard him described as 'inspirational', 'a real gentleman', 'a man ahead of his time', 'a truly good man' and 'the most Christian man in Ireland'. Without exception, everyone was more than willing to do whatever they could to help bring about the publication of this book.

Lena Duff, who was Victor's loyal secretary for many years, told me, 'I always said I would go to the moon for him.' Another person said, 'I would do anything for that man.'

Not only was he kind and charitable, generous and understanding, but Victor Bewley was also incredibly self-effacing. Following his retirement, various members of the family asked him from time to time if he had ever thought of writing his memoirs. His response was always the same. An incredulous look would cross his face and he would ask, 'Who on earth would want to read my memoirs?' My mother, Winifred Murdoch (Victor's eldest daughter), was keen that his life story would be recorded – not necessarily for the general public, but for future generations of the family. Being the only journalist in the clan, I was the obvious one to undertake the task. And when I put it to him, he agreed (much to my surprise and delight) to a series of interviews.

The first interview we did was shortly before his eightieth birthday on 24th May 1992. The project was then dropped until the autumn of 1995, when I was on maternity leave, and we proceeded with a series of interviews. All in all, I ended up with more than ten hours of my grandfather's reminiscences on tape.

I feel totally ashamed that it has taken a further seven years to reproduce his fascinating memories into the form of a book, but motherhood and seven house moves, including several to and fro across the Irish Sea, have conspired against me.

My grandfather answered my questions fully, but in his typical self-effacing manner he rarely offered extra pieces of information about himself: it never crossed his mind that people might be interested to hear them. I would never claim, therefore, that this book offers, in any way, a full account of his life.

With the exception of two chapters, his memoirs are based entirely on my interviews with him. The chapter, 'Love Thy Neighbour as Thyself', comes directly from a typed script I found in his house after his death. It was obviously a talk he gave at some point in the 1970s, but I don't know where or to whom (over the years he was invited to speak to many different groups throughout the country). And some of the information in the chapter on Travellers is extracted from another script that I found.

* * *

Everybody knew Victor Bewley as the face of Bewley's cafes, but few people were aware that, as a child, he had loathed the prospect of going into the business. His childhood ambitions lay in a completely different direction. But, being the eldest son, he had been groomed from the day he was born to take over the firm – an expectation that he resented for many years.

People also knew him as a champion of the Travelling community – never a particularly fashionable cause. What is not so well known is that he was involved in other good causes, too. In the 1970s and 1980s, for instance, he became involved in behind-the-scenes talks with both Republicans and Loyalists and, on one occasion, he brought a message from Dáithí Ó Conaill to the British government.

Some people may wonder what prompted these philanthropic efforts. The chapter, 'Faith, Hope and Love', offers some clues to this conundrum. One thing is certain: faith, for Victor, was not a matter of mere words, but something he translated into action. His life would suggest that, though the Christian faith cannot be verified by logic, it can, perhaps, be demonstrated by example.

Although my grandfather often made media appearances and was frequently invited to give talks, usually on the subject of Travellers, he never sought publicity for himself. In fact, he found it very difficult to appear in the public eye because, throughout his life, he suffered from chronic shyness.

Periods of his life were very bleak and he described some parts as 'undiluted hell'. Victor Bewley did not go in for exaggeration – he believed in speaking the truth plainly – so when he used terms like this I knew he really meant it.

* * *

There are some areas I completely forgot to ask my grandfather about, like his prison work. He started visiting prisoners a long time before he became involved with the Travelling community.

Also, I never asked him about his involvement in The Religious Society of Friends. He was an elder and, over the years, he served on a wide range of committees. In 1953 he was clerk of Yearly Meeting – a position which, in a denomination with no clergy, is the nearest there is to a 'top job'.

He also served on the committees of a number of Quaker schools – namely, Rathgar Junior School, Drogheda Grammar School and Newtown School, Waterford. Again, I didn't ask him about this.

Then there were the things I never knew about – interests that I only came to learn about after his death. I never knew, for example, that he used to bring disadvantaged young people away on camping trips or that he invited children from Derry to camp on his farm.

Neither did I know that he had been on the founding committee of The Rehab Group. In fact, so little did he talk about his interests that no member of the family knew about this particular concern until a research student recently rang my mother looking for further information. Rehab confirmed that Victor had indeed been on the original committee formed in 1949, although in those days it operated under the unwieldy title, The Central Committee for the Rehabilitation of Tuberculous. Its initial meetings were held in Bewley's, Westmoreland Street.

There are many people around who know much more about Victor Bewley than I do. At family gatherings he tended to sit in a corner, quietly watching, listening and taking everything in. He asked questions, but rarely offered any information about himself – only when asked.

It was my grandmother, Winnie Bewley, I used to have long chats with, but she sadly passed away suddenly in the middle of the night on 23rd July 1992. I was inter-railing around Europe at the time and it was the one time in my life that I could not be contacted. I therefore missed her funeral.

It must be said that Winnie was a huge help and support to Victor over the years – without her, he may not have achieved half of what he did. He was a cautious driver and she worried about him driving to meetings in different parts of the country. Often these went on till late in the evening and, during them, Victor frequently met with vitriol and vehement opposition to his work with Travellers. My grandmother often accompanied him on these trips to lend her support and to share the driving.

Some of Victor Bewley's altruistic projects must have had a direct impact on her. I sometimes wonder how she felt when he suggested inviting Travellers and, later, a former prisoner to live on their farm. And how did she feel when, after the war, he invited an orphan boy called Franz, who had been found wandering the streets of Berlin, to come and live with them? After all, Winnie already had their own three young children – Winifred, Rachel and Heather – to look after. And what was it like to have Sunday evenings by the fire interrupted by an unexpected knock on the door from a member of the IRA?

Of course, my grandmother was missed terribly by all of us after her death and there was a painful gap at the dinner table thereafter. However, I did appreciate the opportunity it gave me to talk to Victor more than I had ever done before.

During our series of interviews in 1995 we developed a lovely routine. I would arrive at the farm near Brittas, County Dublin, in time for 'elevenses' and we would settle into comfortable armchairs, which faced out the window and overlooked the Dublin mountains. After one or two hours of interview, my grandfather would be quite tired and we would finish 'work' for the day.

I was always invited to stay for lunch. Victor was impressively domesticated and we would usually eat something delicious made with vegetables grown on the farm. People may be surprised to know that Victor Bewley was a whizz in the kitchen: he made a wicked vegetable curry! And for years he made his own bread and butter.

Throughout his house there were treasured items made by Travellers, which had been given to him over the years as tokens of thanks. There was a beautiful replica of a traditional barrel caravan in the living room, a copper storm lamp in the hall and a multi-coloured crocheted throw on his bed.

* * *

From start to finish it has been a joy and a privilege to work on this book. But it has also been a challenge. Not the actual writing of it, but I found some of my grandfather's words hugely challenging.

He never went in for preaching, but he could be hugely thought-provoking in a rather uncomfortable kind of way. Although he never said as much, I suspect he believed in quietly afflicting the comfortable as well as comforting the afflicted.

I hope that everyone who reads his memoirs will not only enjoy doing so, but will also find themselves challenged. After all, change comes about as the result of being challenged, not from being complacent.

Victor Bewley left the world a better place than he found it. And now it is our turn to do the same.

Fiona Murdoch
August 2002

FAMILY

ONE

A SHELTERED UPBRINGING

I think I must have had a tremendous wish not to be born. My mother was in labour for three days before I finally entered the world on 24 May 1912. My mother never forgot the experience and years later she told me that the doctors had poked around inside her with various instruments and that when I had come out my face was just like a ball of pulp. She thought I would grow up terribly disfigured.

I was born at home which was quite usual in those days. Home was Danum – a thirty-acre farm on Zion Road, Rathgar, where The High School now stands. At that time the Dublin suburbs ended at Rathmines and Danum was in the middle of the countryside.

My father, Ernest Bewley, was fifty-two when I was born. It was his second marriage. He had attended Stranongate School in Yorkshire where he may have met his first wife, Bertha Ann Clark, who was from Doncaster in the north of England. Her health had always been delicate and the wedding had, in fact, been delayed for some years because she wasn't very strong. They were married for eighteen years before Bertha died in 1908, leaving no children.

My father had built Danum – named after the Roman word for Doncaster – in 1900. After Bertha's death, he was left on his own in a big house with only two St Bernard dogs for company. They would lie down beside where he sat in front of the fire in the evenings.

Two years later he married my mother, Susan Emily Clarke. Also from Doncaster, she was a first cousin of his first wife. Susan's parents were missionaries in Madagascar for many years, although when she was born they were back in England on holiday. When she was three months old the time came for them to return overseas. In those days, of course, when you went away you went for a long time because it took three months to get there by ship.

On the journey my mother took ill and she didn't respond to treatment. The ship's doctor said she would die unless she was given some fresh milk. The ship stopped at the next port so that a goat and some fodder could be purchased: my mother had a fresh supply of milk for the rest of the journey and she recovered.

When the family returned to England nine years later my mother spoke fluent Malagasy and only faltering English. I think those early years shaped her life in many ways. She was a very simple woman with a simple lifestyle, but she was also a woman of action. After discussing a particular issue, she would say to us, 'Well then, what are we going to do about it?'

She was a nurse and well used to facing the practicalities of life. She trained as what in those days was called a mental nurse, but now is called a psychiatric nurse. She used to say with some humour that her training was a great help in bringing up her children.

She was a great mother to us. She was entirely devoted to bringing us up and looking after our father who had a very strong personality. He was a real hard worker and a man of great energy and ideas.

My mother had respect for people who were quite different from herself and she accepted people as they were without putting them into stereotypes. Her attitude in that respect affected us. For instance, I was never conscious of colour being a bar when I was growing up. It was only later on that I discovered that colour was a bar for some people. Personally, I find it very interesting to meet people of different types and different backgrounds. I remember the first coloured man who came to our house when I was a boy. We looked forward to him coming and we welcomed him as an interesting visitor rather than looking down on him. I grew up feeling that differences were a point of interest rather than a cause for division and I think that's very important in religious, political and social life. Indeed, in the whole of life. There is more openness of mind and acceptance of the differences among people now, thank goodness.

My parents were loving and wise. They were very good parents who were genuinely fond of us. We were a happy family. You take that for granted when you are young, but later when you realise all the unhappiness there is in the world you appreciate it.

★ ★ ★

I was a shy, apprehensive boy and I harboured a deep-rooted fear of meeting people in large numbers. This fear has stayed with me for my whole life.

One of my earliest memories was during the 1916 Easter Rising. I was four years old at the time and I was rushed into a Lower Mount Street nursing home one day with appendicitis. On the way to the nursing home I said to my mother, 'I do wish they would stop that hammering'. I didn't know it at the time, but it was the sound of gunfire.

My mother told me years later that she could hear bullets rattling off the roof during the operation to remove my appendix. I don't remember that. What I do remember is lying on the operating table screaming my head off with terror when suddenly a thing like an inverted football was placed over my face and I blotted out. Now, of course, I realise that I was being given an anaesthetic.

I remember lying in the ward later when the door opened and a group of people came in – probably a doctor and several nurses – and one of them was carrying a tray holding bottles of medicines. I was in a room with all these strangers and it was very traumatic.

My mother stayed in the hospital with me for four days and, because the city was surrounded, she had no contact with the family at Danum. Nobody was allowed in or out of the city, but she managed to get a message to the family eventually to let them know that the operation had been a success.

I can remember being at home after the operation and playing outside with the others, wondering whether it mattered if I got knocked about after the operation. I suppose I'd been treated as if I was in cotton wool for a while after I came out of hospital.

Years later my father referred to the surgeon who had done the operation. He said to me, 'Your friend, Mr So-and-so, Victor.'

'My friend? You mean my enemy,' I replied.

'Oh no, I mean your friend. He saved your life, you know.'

Until that moment I had never thought of the surgeon as anything but an enemy – somebody who was wicked and whom I dreaded. It wasn't until that moment that I realised that he had, of course, saved my life. And perhaps he had saved my life at the risk of his own because it was a very disturbed time in the city and he could have been shot.

It took me years to get over the experience – in fact, I have never got over it completely. And as a result I have always dreaded meeting large numbers of strangers. Whenever I go to meet a large crowd of people there is still something affecting `me. Although I have never got over it, I have learnt to live with it now, thank goodness.

* * *

I was six years old when the war was over. I can remember climbing over the railings at the front of the house with my brothers and sisters shouting, 'Hip, hip, hooray! The Germans ran away!'

Even though we said that, I don't think we realised anything like the horror it was. There was no doubt but that we lived a very sheltered life at Danum. We had heard of poverty and deprivation, but it was very remote from us.

It was a very happy childhood spent in beautiful surroundings. I remember it was a lovely vista looking out from the house: you could see the flowerbeds, the grass tennis courts and then a line of trees with the mountains behind them.

Our whole family life was sheltered in a very beautiful setting and, with four of us born in quick succession, there were always other children to play with. I was the eldest but one. The eldest, Sylvia, was 11 and a half months older than me. Doris and her twin, Ralph (who died of pnuemonia when he was two and a half), was a year younger and Alfred was a year younger again. There was a gap of six years before the youngest, Joe, was born. He, too, nearly died of pneumonia as a baby.

I have often come across people who have said they had no one to play with when they were growing up, but that was never the case with us. We also had school friends who came and played with us.

We were sheltered, too, in our thinking. My parents had very definite views on right and wrong. We knew where we stood with them and we knew what we should and shouldn't do.

As a child, I wasn't aware of how sheltered and privileged my upbringing was. We had servants in the house, although I don't remember my parents referring to them as servants. They lived in the house with us: they had their own bedrooms, bathroom and easy chairs in the big kitchen. They made our meals and served them. We had a nanny living with us, too. Because there were four of us all in a row my mother was busy looking after one child while she was expecting the next. I remember one nanny in particular called Kate whom I was very fond of. I would totally disapprove of that whole set-up now. I would like to see the differentials in society narrowed.

Much of my childhood was spent outside. There was a large walled garden where my father grew fruit and vegetables. The best produce went into town to be sold in the Bewleys shops; we only ate the damaged fruit and vegetables. I continued this practice after my father died when I was twenty years old.

Father always had very high standards. His motto was, 'The best of everything and that's not good enough.' He produced the fruit and vegetables because he enjoyed doing so and it was convenient having the cafes to take all the produce. There was a great deal of work involved in looking after the grounds and the fruit and vegetables. There were a lot of greenhouses and my father used to aim to bring things in out of season, like tomatoes and strawberries: if you could produce them out of season you could get a much better price for them. Mundane things like carrots and peas were produced for the family, but things like tomatoes were better for selling. These were sold across the counter in the shops along with tea, coffee and buns.

We had Jersey cattle on the farm and the milk from the herd went into town to be used in the cafes. In 1903 my father became the first person to import Jersey cattle into Ireland.[1] Jersey milk was sold in glasses and lots of people came in especially for the milk, particularly if they were anaemic and needed building up. Doctors used to recommend Jersey milk. My father also bred hackney horses which were used for drawing carriages in the days when people didn't have motor cars. When I was a boy, horses and carts were used to bring the produce to the cafes each morning by one of the men who worked on the farm. There were about six or seven people working on the farm then. The cattle were looked after by three men and, of course, all the milking was done by hand in those days.

I wasn't interested in helping with the cows. Alfred was the one who spent time in the cowshed and when our father died he took responsibility for the cattle. We kept a small number of hens and two types of ducks. We knew each individual one and I had a favourite hen – a silver dorking. It was very large and we used her for hatching duck eggs because she could cover so many at a time. One day the time came for her to go because her laying days were over. She was my pet and I couldn't face eating her, so it was arranged that the rest of the family would eat her one evening when I was out visiting a friend and I wouldn't be home for dinner.

I wasn't brought into town much as a boy, but when we did go in on shopping expeditions, my mother would always take us into the cafes for tea and cakes. At that time there were two cafes – one in Westmoreland Street, the other in South Great George's Street. That was always the highlight of our visits to town.

★ ★ ★

Sylvia, Doris, Alfred and I attended Rathgar Junior School the first day it opened in 1919. There were only four other pupils that day, although the numbers grew over time.[2] There were two very dedicated teachers at the time. They were Isabel Douglas, who had trained as a Froebel teacher in England (Froebel was a new approach towards education in those days), and Molly Fayne, a born teacher who loved the things I loved, like nature. I never remember school being anything but a pleasure. Learning was widening my horizons and sparking off interests. I was particularly interested in nature, geography and painting. I was never good at sport. I wasn't built for running and the only sport I was ever good at was swimming. There was a great group of pupils and starting off in the wider world that way was a tremendous help to me. I wasn't troubled with shyness in school because we were all pals together. I remember I enjoyed taking part in the plays we performed at Christmas time. One year I was Hiawatha, another year I was the King of Hearts. I was able to do those things without any fear and to enjoy doing them because I had a sense of security then which was completely different to how I felt when I was older. Throughout my life I have come across people who suffered at school through fear of some of their teachers or as a result of bullying. I was very fortunate to be spared all of that.

★ ★ ★

My parents were both 'Friends'[3] and we attended Churchtown Meeting on Sunday mornings. It was very small then – only a dozen people. It wasn't until the 1930s that the numbers began to grow. My mother was very regular and strict about it: she always went and we were expected to go too. My father was more ready to sometimes find a reason for not going, although he did go pretty regularly, particularly in his later years. Some weeks there was Sunday School; when there wasn't any Sunday School we brought suitable books to read during meeting for worship.

The hour seemed to go by very slowly when I was a child. There was no clock on the wall in those days, but I knew when we were almost halfway through meeting because a train used to go past on the track behind the meeting house at twenty-five past eleven. And I knew meeting was almost finished when another train went past at five to twelve (meeting was over at twelve!).

Both my parents had a very strong faith, bordering on what you might call the liberal evangelical tradition, although I don't really like putting labels on people because they never really fit. My mother had a profound belief in prayer and her views were probably more cut and dry than my father's – that may have been as a result of her days in Madagascar.

They encouraged us to talk about spiritual matters and we always had Bible readings twice a day as a family. In the morning when breakfast was finished and before anybody had left the table, my father would read a passage from the Old Testament and from Daily Light; in the evening, after dinner, he would read from the New Testament. It was a great way of getting to know different parts of the Bible. We would then kneel down in a circle and say together a verse from scripture or a hymn before saying the Lord's Prayer.

★ ★ ★

My happiest childhood memories are of being outside on the farm and of being on holidays in Greystones. My parents used to rent a cottage there for a month during the summer holidays. It was near the sea and the beach was perfectly safe for swimming. We swam off the rocks as well as the shore and we used to go fishing, mainly for pollack. We had a boat that we rowed in the early days until my father bought an outboard engine.

The highlight of the holidays was going on trips in the car to places like Glendalough. I always loved the countryside and beautiful scenery, as did my parents.

We never went on holiday anywhere else and, although I loved it so much, a time came when I grew discontented and longed to see other places. Connemara was a place I'd heard about and would have loved to have gone to see. We'd got into the routine of going to Greystones, however, and my father was hitting seventy and he didn't need to break new horizons like I did. So we never went.

★ ★ ★

After World War I many Protestant families left Ireland because they didn't want to live under the new government. I don't think my family ever considered leaving. I never heard my parents talk about it and, anyway, my father's roots were much too deep to consider leaving. Even though my father was a unionist, it was always assumed that our future was in Dublin. He said quite frankly that, with the exodus that was taking place after the war, the country would go to the dogs. His opinion had nothing to do with bigotry – he wasn't bigoted. He just didn't believe people here were capable of running the country. He didn't live long enough to see that he was wrong.

Notes

1. Ernest Bewley became the first president of the Jersey Cattle Society of Ireland, a post later held by his two sons, Alfred and Joe, and later still by Joe's son, Roger.

2. Rathgar Junior School on Grosvenor Road was founded by a Quaker, Isabel Douglas, and the school still has Quaker connections. Victor Bewley's youngest daughter, Heather Bewley, has been its headmistress since 1981. There are currently 156 pupils enrolled in the school. Before attending RJS Victor spent a couple of years at a school on Frankfort Avenue run by a Miss Tuckey.

3. 'Friends' is an abbreviated term for the Christian denomination known as The Religious Society of Friends (or Quakers). Their services are called meetings for worship and are held in meeting houses as opposed to churches. For more information see Appendix.

TWO

A CAREFUL GROOMING

I was sent to Bootham School in York when I was twelve years old. It was my first time away from home and it nearly broke my heart.

As the time drew near to leave home I was filled with dread. When I got there I hated it, even though my cousin, Bill Bewley, was there too. My sister, Sylvia, was at The Mount, also in York, and I saw her every Sunday after meeting for worship.[1]

I had nothing against Bootham – it was a good school and I grew to like it – but while I was there I decided it was a mistake for me to have been sent there. If I was going to spend the rest of my life in Ireland I thought I should have been sent to school in Ireland where I would have formed friendships which could have continued after school.

At that time my parents, along with other Friends in Ireland, felt that Quaker schools in England were better than Irish ones and a steady flow of Quaker children were sent to schools there. Newtown School in Waterford was open, but it was not as developed then as it is now. My father had been to another Quaker school in Yorkshire, Stranongate, and my mother and her sisters had gone to the girls' school, The Mount.

I was reasonably hard working at Bootham, but I was never a brilliant academic. I was surprised one year when I was asked to take part in the Christmas play. It had never occurred to me to even think about auditioning for it. I landed the leading role in a Shakespeare drama and, the following year, I took part in Sheridan's *The Rivals*.

I was never a loner. Always through my life I have been able to make friends, thank goodness. I had not a large number of friends, but I had friends and they were very good friends. We had a lot in common, particularly art. We only had art classes up until the end of second form, but after that I spent a lot of my free time painting; there was an art room where you could go and paint for as long as you liked in your spare time. There were three or four of us who liked doing that. I painted mainly landscapes from my memories of the Irish countryside. I could never stand painting still life.

One picture I painted was of a sunset over hills and my father had it framed and hung it in the drawing room at Danum. Another was of the cottage where we used to stay in Greystones and it included the cove where we used to bathe. I always enjoyed swimming – it was the only sport I was ever any good at. I remember one day at Bootham a master insisted I get out of the pool even though I wanted to keep going. I had swum two miles, but I felt sure I could do more.

I liked French and I used to read novels in French. In those days I thought I was called to be a missionary in Madagascar and one of the languages I would have needed was French. I had always been interested in what my mother had to say about Madagascar. She had a sister who was a missionary there when I was growing up and, when I met her, I thought she came across as a very strict person. But I was very fond of her and I listened to everything she said.

My concept of being a missionary was to relieve people from living in fear and to help in situations where people were socially deprived. I was interested in educational work and growing crops. I haven't lived my life regretting I wasn't a missionary. It came to me that if I had anything of value to give to my fellow human beings I should be able to do it here without having to go elsewhere to do it.

If I were not to be a missionary, I would like to have been an artist or a concert pianist. I was very absorbed in music and painting – particularly oil painting, which I started when I was at Bootham. My father was a great encouragement: he encouraged us to develop and express ourselves. He took a great interest in my painting and he was very fond of music.

I realised later that I hadn't really the ability in either to make a living for myself, let alone my family. It was a mad hope to be a concert pianist: there was never the slightest possibility of it because I never had that kind of ability. Although I knew I would never be able to fulfil these dreams, the ambitions never left me and I have kept up my interests in playing the piano and painting throughout my life.[2]

Before I went to Bootham I had two music teachers. The first one came to the house and we visited the other one, Mrs Yoakley, at her house. When I came back from Bootham I went back to her for some years. I had a piano teacher at Bootham, but I didn't like his way of teaching and I instinctively felt I wasn't getting far with him. I told this to my parents in one of my letters home and that one day in exasperation the teacher had said to me about a particular piece of music, 'You know, you'll never learn to play that'. I turned to him and said, 'Well, it's your job to teach it to me'. I asked my parents to write to the headmaster and ask him to change my music teacher. They did. And I got on well with the new teacher.

Most nights after dinner, when we were all at home, I would play the piano and that was a tremendous help to my music. Usually we took turns to play, but I played more than my brothers and sisters because I was more interested in it. I enjoyed playing and my father enjoyed listening. I practised hard at things that he liked so that I would be good enough to play them. I liked Chopin best – also Beethoven and Mozart. I took exams at the Royal Academy of Music.

After my father's death I was very preoccupied with the business, but I kept the piano up for a while. I missed his presence, though, knowing that he was enjoying listening.

* * *

When I finished school at the age of seventeen I came straight back to Ireland. We spent our holidays, as usual, in Greystones, and in September I went to Newcastle-on-Tyne to stay with a school friend. On my return home, it was decided that I would start work in Bewley's on October 1st.

I grew up feeling that the sole purpose of my existence was to carry on the firm. I don't blame my father for that and he never specifically said it, but it was something I resented. I was always very interested in hearing anything about the firm that he told us, but not from the point of view of my becoming involved. I never wanted to go into the business. My father must have been aware that I had never expressed any interest in going into the firm. I remember one time I made some comment about entering the business and he said to me, 'Well, you have never said that you would like to go into it'. I think he must have been waiting for years for me to say this and I had never said it. In the end I didn't say it because I didn't have to. After all, I had no choice in the matter.

I had been in the firm a year when my father became ill with dropsy – a disease in which watery fluid collects in the body. He rallied a bit, but never fully recovered. He died eight months later in August 1932. My father and his friend, George Acheson Overend, who was our solicitor and a director of Bewley's Cafes, had wanted me to go to Trinity College Dublin. I never wanted to go, but they enrolled me anyway to do Business Studies. It was bad enough having to go into the business, but the thought of going to Trinity was even worse. I felt it was definitely not for me: partly because of my shyness, but also because I reckoned it was too academic a place for me. I pictured all the students being good at sport and other things that wouldn't have interested me.[3]

As it turned out, Trinity became completely out of the question with my father's death. I already had a tutor appointed to me and I was absolutely delighted when I had to go and tell him that I wouldn't need him because I would not be going to Trinity after all.

* * *

On three different occasions when I was a young adult I dreamt that I was driving around Danum in a high-powered car.[4] Each time I dreamt I was coming down the drive towards the gate and that as I approached the gate the car slowed down, but the gate never opened and I never went through it.

I didn't think anything of it at the time, but later I thought this was something in me that was seeking a wider horizon and new experiences.[5] That was possibly the beginning of my urge to move out – not only to move away from Danum, but also to broaden my thinking and experiences in order to widen my horizons.

In 1926 my father bought a Bentley: it wasn't his first car, but it became his great pride and joy. I drove him in it sometimes, but I didn't like driving it.[6] There weren't many Bentleys about and it was quite a status symbol, but I wouldn't go along with that kind of thing. It was very comfortable and a very nice car to be driven in, but it belonged to a very different view of society than mine.

It is hard to say why I developed different views to my parents, but I did from early on. Danum was a beautiful house with beautiful big rooms, but it belonged to another era. Even as a child I thought, 'Why should one family live like this when other families have to live in a single room?' I was never one for accepting things without challenging them. I wouldn't go along with something just for the sake of it and my leaning towards a simple life is something I have always been interested in. I used to take the view that if you adjusted incomes and conditions that society's problems would be solved, but as time went on I realised that was not the case. While I have always considered it important to bring living standards closer together, I realise now that there is more to life than that. There are many more problems in life than just different standards of living – that is only a part of it. I am very much in favour of narrowing the differentials in standards of living. There are far too many people who are living on or below the poverty line and one of the things that saddens me very much is that we have become a selfish society, each of us out to do the best for ourselves. I dislike labels because they tend to create barriers, so I would shy away from the description of 'socialist', and when it comes to elections I prefer to vote for the best candidates rather than along party lines.

Notes

1. Bootham and The Mount are both Quaker boarding schools in York – the former for boys, the latter for girls.
2. On at least one occasion Victor accepted an invitation to display some of his oil paintings as part of an exhibition organised by the Sunday Painters Group.
3. Meanwhile Victor's future wife, Winnie Burne (my grandmother), would have dearly loved to have gone to Trinity, as she often told me wistfully during my four years there. She couldn't understand why her parents were so dead set against it, insisting on her entering employment straight after school. They hadn't told her that her father was, in fact, critically ill with diabetes. He died three months after she started work.
4. It is perhaps interesting to note that throughout his life Victor was, in fact, a slow and cautious driver and he never showed any interest in powerful cars!
5. Winifred Murdoch reckons her father had an interest in dreams throughout his life. He made a point of telling her about some of the dreams he had during his last year of life; she wondered if these referred to his imminent departure from this life.
6. Victor's younger sister Doris, on the other hand, loved to drive her father's Bentley. She was delighted to find herself behind its wheel again in August 1999 after it was purchased by a friend of the family in Kildare, Bernard O'Gorman. In the 1940s the Bentley had been exported to England and then to South Africa where a Mr Loney spent twenty years restoring it to its present pristine condition. In 1990 it was seen worldwide by television viewers when a number of dignitaries appeared in it during the celebrations which followed Nelson Mandela's release from prison.

THREE

COURTSHIP, MARRIAGE AND FAMILY LIFE

The first time I met Winnie Burne was at a children's party at the Quaker meeting house in Rathmines where Winnie's family attended meeting for worship on Sundays. We were both ten years old at the time.

We were sitting around having our tea when a message was passed down the line of children saying, 'Winnie Burne says to tell Victor Bewley to drink his tea without putting his nose in the cup'. She was only pulling my leg!

The next time we met was when I returned to Dublin from Bootham and an older Quaker organised a party for all the Quakers in Dublin who had just left school. There were seven or eight of us and Winnie was there too. We both started attending the Dublin Young Friends Group that met every Monday evening in Eustace Street Meeting House. We saw a lot of each other at other Friends' events too. I remember one Saturday afternoon in 1930 soon after the death of her father, Richard, I called over to her house and I took Winnie and her mother, Frances, for a run in my father's car to Glendalough. It wasn't until a couple of years later – around the time of my own father's death – that we started going together. I remember we both attended a Young Friends conference in Bangor, Co. Down, and out of the crowd milling around she came up to me and spoke to me in a very friendly way. It was then that I first felt that she was someone special.

We started going for walks together and we went to the pictures, to the theatre and to concerts. I used to cycle into town to work[1] and I'd stay on late for the Young Friends Group meetings on Monday nights. I used to walk Winnie home to Terenure where she lived with her mother. I pushed my bicycle as far as her house and then rode the rest of the way home.

In the summer Young Friends played tennis, sometimes at Danum and sometimes at other Friends' houses. After one evening at Danum in 1935 people were gradually drifting home as it was getting dark and, finally, there was only the two of us left. We went for a walk around the farm and when we reached the bridge that went over the mill race the two of us ended up standing there chatting for ages. And that's where I proposed to her at dusk. We married two years later on 9th June 1937 in Churchtown Meeting House. We were both twenty-seven years old.

Winnie gave up work when we got married – it was usual in those days for women to do this. She had been working in the Currency Commission on Dame Street. We spent a week on honeymoon in Roundstone, Co. Galway. We had been there for a few days on a previous holiday and we had both fallen in love with it.

There was a Friends World Conference in Swarthmore College in Pennsylvania three months later and we were asked by Yearly Meeting's Committee if we would like to go, with a group of other Irish Friends, as representatives from Ireland. It would never have occurred to us to go if we had not been asked to go as representatives and we agreed to attend. One day in September we left on a Sunday morning from Cobh and it took a week to get to America by ship. We returned on the Aquitania which landed at Southampton. That was a wonderful experience.

After the week-long conference we travelled to New York. I asked the board in Bewley's for an extra week's holiday (in those days we had three weeks' annual leave) to look around cafes, bakeries and other businesses of a similar type to ourselves. They gladly gave their permission.

I don't remember which floor we were on in the hotel but, my goodness, with the heat and the noise I didn't think I'd ever get to sleep the first night. I thought it was a dreadful place, New York. But by the end of the week we'd got used to it and I wouldn't have minded spending another week there. But I still wouldn't like to live there. We saw the Statue of Liberty and we went up the Empire State Building and we did a few other things we felt we ought to do as tourists. All in all, it was a nice trip.

We slept in separate beds for the first few months of our marriage. We did this to ensure Winnie wouldn't fall pregnant before we returned from our trip to America. There was no contraception available in those days.

We spent the first seventeen years of our marriage living in the top half of Danum. For the first year my mother lived downstairs with Alfred and Joe – Sylvia and Doris were already married. When Alfred married Mary Sessions from Yorkshire the following year mother and Joe moved out and Alfred and Mary lived in the downstairs apartment. We bought a house on Rostrevor Road for mother and Joe – their garden could be entered through a door in the wall from Danum. The door is still there, although I imagine it is never used now.

When Winnie and I left Danum in 1954 our friends, Erwin and Lisl Strunz, moved in and lived there for the next two years. We decided to move out because the house was too big to keep up. I remember the last estimate we got for painting the outside of the house and the outbuildings was £500. It was then that we realised it was beyond our pockets and that it was time to go. It was the expense of staying there that made us leave. In 1956 the firm bought Ballyowen, a farm near Clondalkin. Alfred and Mary moved there with the stock from Danum.[2]

* * *

As a small boy, I'd always had a picture in my mind of a whitewashed cottage with a little farm around it. I used to do paintings of this place and I would have some fields with cows in them and some hens. I dreamed of living somewhere like that, but I never thought I actually would.

However, before we moved out of Danum we bought 11 acres of land near Brittas, Co. Dublin, from a Friend, Douglas Harrison. We told an architect what kind of house we wanted and that it had to be no more than 1,400 square feet to qualify for a grant. We didn't want anything large, anyway – it was all part of living a simple life. He produced a drawing that we liked and that is how our new home, Corrymeela, came to be designed for us. It was perfectly adequate for our needs. We moved here on 8 April 1954 and we have enjoyed living here ever since.

When we came here there were two old men living in a cottage on adjacent land. They weren't getting any younger and they weren't getting any better in health and they said to me several times that when they died they would like me to buy their cottage and land. So I did. That increased the size of the farm to thirty acres.[3]

* * *

I have tremendously enjoyed being a father and a grandfather.[4] I think of life now if I hadn't had that experience and I think how much I would have missed. I don't know if I ever thought about what values I should pass on to my children. I've thought more about what values I should live by and I think that if there's anything worth passing on, it will be absorbed. And if it's not worth passing on, then it's better if it's forgotten. I would never have wanted to impose my ideas on my children.

For a certain length of time after we were married we continued my parents' tradition of Bible readings after breakfast and dinner. But when the pattern of life changed as the children grew older, and they were coming and going at different times to their various activities, we decided, with some reluctance, to discontinue.

I had made up my mind while I was still at school that if I ever had children they would go to school in Ireland – it had been a mistake to send us to England as we didn't live there. What I feared would happen did happen: the friends I made at school – and I made some very good friends – some of them I never saw again and most of them I saw only occasionally.

Winnie had not been to boarding school whereas I had.[5] We thought long and hard about it before deciding to send our girls to Newtown School in Waterford. There is no Quaker secondary school in Dublin and we wanted our children to go to a Quaker co-educational school. We valued the Quaker values and I would have felt confined sending them to a non-Quaker school and I wouldn't have wanted my children to feel that.

I have an open mind on boarding school now and, if I were to make the decision today, I think I would probably come down in favour of a day school in Dublin. You can argue it both ways – it's such a big hunk out of your life at a very formative age and yet boarding school is such a great experience when you get over the initial shock. It was a tremendous wrench for me to go to boarding school, but Bootham was a good school and I was happy there after the opening weeks.

I never expected any of my daughters to go into the firm. As I've said, I felt very strongly that I was brought into this world to carry on the business and I feared this and I resented it in a quiet, smouldering kind of way. I didn't want any of my children to go through that so I never assumed that they might want to go in or that they would go in.

Nevertheless, I was pleased when Rachel decided to go to The Dublin College of Catering, Cathal Brugha Street. And, once I knew it was her clear decision to enter the firm, I told her everything I could to help. She became manageress of Westmoreland Street with specific responsibility for three other cafes and to the bakery canteen. In the early 1970s she was made a company director and she later became manageress of Grafton Street café.[6]

★ ★ ★

It wasn't until after my father's death that I finally visited Connemara – a place I had heard about and I had dreamed of visiting. The first time I went I was twenty and I went with my school friend, Harold Johnson. We went for a week and we stayed in farmhouses in Recess and Leenane. We spent all day on our bicycles and I loved it. We were chatting one evening and I thought Harold was showing an unnecessary interest in my younger sister, Doris. Finally I got it out of him that he was keen on her. One night after we got home I heard her on the phone to him and, although I can't remember what she was saying, I realised the feelings were reciprocated.[7]

Following our honeymoon in Roundstone in Connemara, Winnie and I returned there almost every year until 1952 when we bought a cottage slightly further north on Errislannan peninsula, near Clifden. The two or three years we didn't go to Connemara we chose to visit Kerry and Donegal, instead. They are very beautiful counties too.

A lot of people have the experience that a certain place is special for them and Connemara became my own personal favourite corner of Ireland. It somehow has a character of its own. It's just the place to relax, but it is also full of interest with its beautiful countryside and its many different flowers. I used to enjoy painting a lot on my holidays. Different places are like different people: they each have their own character. I'm trying to think of a poem I learnt at school. It goes like this…

> God gave all men all earth to love
> But since our hearts are small
> Ordained for each one spot to prove
> Beloved over all.

Travel has never interested me that much. I've been on very happy and interesting travels, but it never occurred to me to go on a trip unless somebody else either invited me or organised it. We went to Paris a couple of times to attend a catering exhibition; Rachel accompanied us on one of those trips.

Usually our travels came out of the blue. We were at home one Sunday evening in 1956 when Harold rang up and asked if we would like to go on a trip to Chamonix in Switzerland. We went through a process of wondering would we, wouldn't we, before deciding that we would. So we rang back and said we'd go. Harold said to come over straightaway and he'd give us more details. We ended up having a marvellous three weeks divided between Chamonix, Interlaken and Grindelwald.

We fell in love with Grindelwald and when our three daughters clubbed together in 1979 to give us a cheque to put towards a special trip we asked ourselves where we would like to go. We agreed that because we had such happy memories of Switzerland we would like to return there. We plumped for a hotel in Grindelwald and we had a lovely time.

In 1960 Winnie and I went to Kenya on a coffee-tasting trip. It was arranged by a party involved in the coffee trade to meet some of the growers. I had a telephone call from a man in London and he was telling me that this trip had been organised and he asked if Winnie and I would like to go. I wasn't very keen at first – I'm not sure why – so I said I would think about it. We had about three days to make up our minds. I said it to Winnie when I got home that evening and she said there was no way she was interested: she didn't like flying and she wouldn't fly to Kenya or anywhere else. In the end, I don't know how we sorted it out, but we decided we would both go.[8]

It turned out to be a magnificent experience and full of interest for both of us the whole time. We used every minute we had. There were times off when the organised trip hadn't anything arranged. We were based in Nairobi and I remember that during one of our free times we got a train from Nairobi to Mombassa on the coast. We had a meal on the train before going to sleep and when we woke up the next day we were in Mombassa. We had a contact there who arranged for a guide to drive us around the city and down to the docks to see the dhows and all the different goings-on there. We also visited a mosque. That was a wonderful trip.

So we did travel a bit, but it was always out of the blue like that.

Notes

1. Victor rode his bicycle into town every day for twenty-five years. He didn't start driving to work until 1954 when he moved to Corrymeela near Brittas, Co, Dublin.

2. In the early 1940s the firm bought Knocksedan – a farm near Dublin airport where Lord Edward Fitzgerald once lived and which Sean O'Casey mentions in his play, *Shadow of a Gunman*. Joe lived there by himself for a couple of years and then with his wife, Dorothy Manico, following their marriage in 1943. In 1970 Ballyowen was compulsorily acquired by Dublin Corporation and the firm bought Shingled House in Leixlip, Co. Kildare, where Alfred and Mary moved. Meanwhile Moyvalley – a farm of some 600 acres in Co. Kildare – was bought and the stock from both Knocksedan and Ballyowen was moved there. There were 300 Jersey cattle in total. Joe and Dot lived in Moyvalley until it was sold in 1984 to ease the company's cash flow problems.

3. Victor proceeded to fill the fields with cows and hens just as he had imagined in his pictures. Over the years he also kept ducks, geese, cats and dogs and he grew a variety of fruit and vegetables. He aimed to lead as self-sufficient a lifestyle as possible and he brought excess produce into town for sale in Bewley's shops and cafes – primarily milk, cream, eggs, carrots and rhubarb.

4. Winifred was born in 1939, Rachel in 1943 and Heather in 1945. Winifred was the only daughter to have children. Following her marriage to Brian Murdoch in 1961, Hazel was born in 1963, Peter in 1965 and I was born in 1969. I have no doubt Victor enjoyed being a great- grandfather, too, but none of his great-grandchildren were born at the time of this interview. He met five of his great-grandchildren before he died. Katie Murdoch, the eldest, was born on 28th March 1994, Amy Carmichael on 22nd September 1994, Ruari Williamson on 30th January 1996, Zoe Carmichael on 19th April 1996 and Lucy Murdoch on 22nd September 1996. Niamh Carmichael was born on 18th June 1999, just three weeks after Victor died.

5. Winnie attended Alexandra College, Dublin from 1922 to 1929.

6. Rachel Bewley-Bateman also spent five years in catering in Britain, France and Switzerland. She retired from Bewley's in 1984 and later went into business with her husband, John Bateman.

7. Victor 'gave away' Doris on the occasion of her marriage to Harold Johnson in 1936 at Churchtown Meeting House.

8. Winifred remembers her mother talking to her before the trip as though they would never see each other again. Despite an intense fear of flying, Winifred says her mother loved to travel.

BUSINESS

FOUR

THE BEWLEY
HERITAGE

The Bewleys arrived in Ireland at the turn of the sixteenth century, fleeing religious persecution in England.[1] They first settled in the midlands, only coming up to Dublin towards the end of the eighteenth century.

It was my grandfather, Joshua, who started the business. The earliest record we have is from the 1840s: I found an old ledger with that date on it, but how long he was in business before that we cannot know for certain. He started off in premises consisting of three houses on Sycamore Street, just off Dame Street and beside the Olympia Theatre, although in those days it was known as Sycamore Alley. He dealt mainly in tea and sugar and a small amount of coffee; he also sold oriental vases and ornaments. His eldest son, Charles, was involved in the early days and my father, Ernest, went into the business after leaving school in 1876.

My father was paid a shilling a week which didn't really suit him because he was a hard worker and good at business. He felt that his father was not a good businessman and that the firm would not get very far. After some time he left and set up a poultry farm. His decision to leave was not the result of a row, but because he felt there simply wasn't room for the three of them in the business. Charles, however, was in poor health. He suffered from asthma and, after his doctor advised him to move to a warmer climate, he emigrated to New Zealand where he settled and married. Joshua asked my father to go back into business with him; my father said he would if he was paid the same as his brother had been paid. My grandfather agreed.

By that time he was operating at 13 South Great Georges Street which he had bought in 1894. He still dealt in only a small amount of coffee, which he bought by the stone from a cousin, with deliveries being made by horses and drays. On one occasion my father had a disagreement with the cousin. I don't know what it was about, but he made up his mind not to buy coffee from him any longer but from a wholesaler instead. He found he could not buy coffee by the stone from the wholesaler, however: he had to buy a hundredweight at a time. In his own words, he 'shivered in his shoes' in case he would never be able to sell it all. As a means of promoting the sale of this hundredweight of coffee, he started to hold coffee-making demonstrations at the back of the shop in the hopes that people would make a purchase on their way out. His wife, Bertha, made rolls and scones which my father took into town on the back of his bicycle to serve with the coffee. That was how the cafes started. Two years later, in 1896, the café at 10 Westmoreland Street was opened.

In 1900 my father bought 19/20 Fleet Street with the intention of opening a bicycle shop. He was very handy and he could repair anything. He took a partner to work with him in the shop, but he found one day that his partner was unreliable and so dissolved the partnership. He decided to open a café there, instead.

In 1916 he bought 12 Westmoreland Street. It linked up with his Fleet Street premises and he decided to turn the front into a shop and the back into a café.[2]

My father never advertised his business: he believed you should give good quality service and that that should be your only advertisement. He reckoned if the public was pleased with your service that they would come back and support you. It was up to you to get your quality right. However, business in 1916 was poor because of the disturbed times and one day he broke with tradition and placed an advertisement in The Irish Times. The first customer who came into the shop that day said, 'How the mighty have fallen!' My father was so cut to the quick by the remark that he never advertised again.

In 1926 my father changed the name of the firm from Charles Bewley & Co to Bewley's Oriental Cafes Ltd. Not long after that he purchased 78-79 Grafton Street. He spent £45,000 on buying and refurbishing the premises and a further £14,900 on fixtures and fittings before it was finally opened on 27th November 1927.

Notes

1. The Bewley family is French in origin, moving from France to the north of England in the middle ages. Mungo Bewley, Victor's great-great-great grandfather, left Cumberland for Ireland in 1700 and settled in Edenderry, Co Offaly. All the present day Bewleys are descended from him. At that time Quakers in Britain were coming into conflict with the established order, primarily because they refused to take the oath. This refusal barred them from the professions and many chose to go into business, instead. Ireland offered the prospect of religious freedom under the Toleration Act.

2. It was at this time that the bakery started, mainly with confectioners from mainland Europe.

FIVE

A RELUCTANT BUSINESSMAN

I cycled into work on my first day – 1 October 1929. That was something I continued to do for the next twenty-five years.[1] When I arrived at Bewley's, Westmoreland Street, I had no idea what kind of work I was going to do. There had been no discussion at home about what I was going to be doing in the business. I suppose my father had told the secretary I was coming, but I was left standing in the office waiting for him to decide what I was going to do. I felt that I stuck out like a sore thumb and that everyone could see me standing there, like an idiot. Anyway, he eventually decided that I would start off by doing the ordinary office work. My older sister, Sylvia, started work around the same time, but she was doing a secretarial course in the mornings so she only came into work in the afternoons. The two of us started off by doing clerical work.

At each end of the café there was a cash desk where people paid before they left. For some reason my father decided we weren't to learn how to do that. After a while we decided we wanted to do exactly the same as the rest of the staff and I remember asking if we could learn to do the cash desk. My father agreed.

It wasn't long before my father started consciously training me to take over the firm. In a sense, I suppose, he had been training me from the day I was born because he used to talk at home about what was going on in the business.

He soon started training me in tasting the tea and coffee. A row of little bowls was set out in his office upstairs in Westmoreland Street and we dipped our spoons in, tasted, and spat the drink out into a spittoon. We couldn't possibly have drunk it all, it would have been bad for us.

Tastings took place two or three times a week – usually in the first part of the morning, as soon as the coffee had arrived from London on the last leg of its journey. We imported the coffee from Colombia, Kenya and Africa. It was terribly important to keep the tastes similar and if you wanted to change a blend, you had to do it slowly because if the public got used to a taste and then found it one day to be different, they would be upset and feel sure that they were being 'done'. I always enjoyed experimenting with new blends, although I had to be careful to give the public what they wanted – not what I thought they wanted. I had to try and find out what they did want.

We always had some Darjeeling teas – they are the best kind of Indian tea – and I remember one year I got some lovely Darjeeling teas in earlier than usual and I realised that they were arriving in time for Christmas. I was delighted with myself, making up some different kinds of blends. But some people didn't like it: I had changed it too quickly. From that time on I learned to change blends more slowly.

I enjoyed tasting: it was like mixing paints and achieving different colours, tastes and blends. We were always testing for quality, of course. We used to have ten different teas in a blend. There were not so many in coffee – you would have maybe two, three or four different ones until you achieved the kind of flavour you wanted. We used the same basic mix until I left.

After my father died the tastings became my responsibility. When my brother, Alfred, came into the business he did tastings with me for a while. One day in conversation, however, it turned out he was quite keen to become a baker and so he gave up tasting and went to the bakery.[2] Later, when he became more established in the bakery he took up tasting again. Later still, when my nephew, Patrick Bewley, entered the business in 1965, he started tasting too. So there was always two of us at any time who knew what to do.

I always enjoyed the tea and coffee tasting. I also enjoyed dressing the windows; I used to do the ones in Westmoreland Street. That was a form of art, particularly around Christmas time.

* * *

My father was almost seventy when I started work. In those days seventy seemed a lot older than it is now because people didn't live as long then. But he was in good health and I had no idea that he would be gone within a couple of years.

I remember, when I was still at school, my mother wrote to tell us that father was very ill. He did recover, although the illness left him a bit shook, and I don't think he was ever completely himself again afterwards. The opening of Grafton Street in 1927 took a lot out of him, too, which didn't help.

He became ill, this time with dropsy, shortly before Christmas 1931, and he had to have excess fluid in his body removed regularly with a syringe. While he was ill in St James's Hospital some of the senior members of staff visited him every day and kept him informed about the business. I'm not sure at what stage it dawned on me that he might never recover, but he was definitely never the same again. He made a partial recovery in the spring and returned to work on crutches. He soon started going downhill, however, and he died, after eight months of illness, in August 1932.

* * *

Even though I was only twenty, I had already been made a director of the firm. My mother's brother, Dick Clark, was our auditor and he was also a director. So was the firm's solicitor, George Acheson Overend, as was a distant cousin, Tom Bewley. My mother was a director, too, although on paper only – she hadn't a clue about the business. In fact, none of them really knew much about the business.

The opening of the Grafton Street branch five years earlier had left the firm very much in the red and the bank was already pressing for the firm's closure because of its colossal overdraft. Mr Overend and Mr Clark were a strong influence in the firm. Mr Clark felt that they should ask the bank to appoint someone to run the place. Mr Overend, on the other hand, pleaded with the bank to give us a chance. He fought very hard and, in the end, the bank gave us a year to prove ourselves. Mr Overend, with the backing of the staff, approved that I could run the business. Although they felt I could take on the role of managing director there and then, I felt totally inadequate for the job and didn't know how I could possibly do it. I was young and inexperienced and I had no thoughts of becoming MD.

They would have liked me to have become MD straightaway, but they reckoned it would be bad for business to have a boy of twenty running the place. So it was decided that I would continue as a director, but that I wouldn't become MD until I turned twenty-one. So I took over my father's office and I did the work of an MD although I wasn't given the title until the following year. It was ridiculous though: I was totally unsuited to it.

There was nobody who could take me under their wing and show me how to run the business because my father had been doing it all himself. We had a great staff however. There were four senior members of staff, in particular, who were towers of strength to me. They were Theodore Halliday, Elizabeth Cassidy, Isa Hewson and Elizabeth Ward.[3] I was deeply grateful to them for their backing and I valued their experience in the firm. Underlying the idea of common ownership, which I introduced in 1972, was the realisation that there was a resource there to be used both in the senior staff's understanding of the business and in their relationship with other members of staff. I came to see that there should be a team spirit running the show.

We gradually went through the transition period between my father running the business and then me running it. I remember one day I just didn't know what to do, so I took up one of the accounting books I had been keeping up until then to continue on with it. Someone came into the office and saw me: she said that it wasn't suitable work for an MD. She was quite right, of course, but I had only been doing it to fill in an awkward gap. I didn't know what on earth I should have been doing!

I never did do the books again after that and the days soon started filling up. In the beginning it was mostly about listening, without being able to offer any advice. I tried to walk around each of the departments in the three cafes every day. I talked to those in charge and listened to their problems. My father had listened to some of the older staff, too, but I don't know to what extent he had sought their opinions.

Listening to the staff was always important to me. It comes out so often in industrial disputes that there has been no consultation with staff – in other words, no consideration of other people. That was something that was very important to me right from the start. The staff all had their different functions in the firm and I found that very interesting. I enjoyed the opportunities to get to know the staff as people. I also enjoyed getting to know the customers. I got to know a lot of them and I often thought they would be surprised to know how much was known about them by the staff. I don't know how we got all the information.

Some people you never got to know anything much about at all: they may have come in at twelve o'clock for their lunch everyday and you knew them as part of the place, but you never got to know any more about them. But there were others we collected all sorts of information about. I don't mean that we set out to do it: it just happened. Of course, the cafes were a great meeting place. Maud Gonne frequented Bewley's in my early days. She was very dignified and yet a very simple kind of person. I wouldn't have agreed with all of her views, but she was a nice person to talk to.[4]

Bewley's was obviously a place conducive to writers because there was a lot of life milling around, so to speak. Mary Lavin was donkeys' years coming in and I believe she wrote some of her early stories in the cafes. Maeve Binchy became a regular customer when she worked on *The Irish Times*; I can remember her interviewing me for the paper on one occasion.[5]

I noticed changes in the clientele over the years. It was very exclusive in my early days and outside the pocket of a great many people. I deliberately set out to make it accessible to as many people as possible by trying to keep the prices down. My father took a different approach to providing food. Initially he sold only tea, coffee and cakes – although he later offered sausages and eggs too. He was dead against going for a restaurant trade because he said it was much more difficult to make a profit from running a restaurant than from running a café because the staff overheads were much higher.

It was nice to be in a place where you were dealing with the people you were trying to serve. I would find a lot of modern kinds of business terribly boring where you're just signing contracts without ever seeing people.

★ ★ ★

Within a year of my becoming MD we managed to satisfy the bank that the firm was viable after all. Grafton Street stayed in the red until sometime around World War II when it turned the corner,[6] but in my forty-four years as MD in only two years did we fail to make an overall profit. Profit is what the bank wants, of course: at the end of the day it is only figures that matter to them.

Usually the profit level was very small, as was the loss very small in those two years. The first loss was fairly early on, but we had already had time to show the bank what we could do. It was in the nature of only a few pounds – £10 or something like that. The other year was 1974 when the loss was marginally more, but not a huge amount. Our one great goal in the beginning was to get rid of the overdraft. We worked hard to do that and we were very careful how we spent money. We never saved money by cutting staff though. We only ever cut staff once in my time and it was in this way. The bakers and confectionery staff were the only staff who were in a union and new boys coming in to learn the trade were apprentices for the first four years. They were paid something very nominal in the beginning, but that soon increased and, after four years, they were qualified confectioners and received full wages. It was the practice in most bakeries that when the apprentices' time was up they would leave and you would take in another batch of apprentices in their place – apprentices were cheaper, of course, than qualified staff. I remember one time an apprentice had served his time and I let him know it was time for him to leave. Even though this was normal practice, he was very sore about it. It was the first time it occurred to me that there was anything odd about the practice: up until that point I had just accepted that it was the correct thing to do. After that I never dismissed an apprentice unless we absolutely had to. And in no other department in my time did we ever dismiss anyone.

I remember when we introduced our first self-service section on the second floor of Grafton Street in December 1969. Part of the idea behind it, naturally, was to reduce staff, but we went through a transition period in which all staff were kept on. We had a large number of women employees and the custom at that time was for women to give up work when they got married. That was never queried: they didn't have to leave, but it is what all women did at the time. In later years some stayed until they became pregnant, leaving at some point before the birth. So we knew the staff would gradually reduce in numbers and we got down to the right number in time.

I never advertised Bewley's shops or cafes. Like my father, I believed that customers would return so long as they were satisfied with your service. It was a long time before we even advertised any job vacancies. Usually people were employed through word of mouth or personal recommendations. We had enough people sending us applications and I always kept them. At first, I didn't always acknowledge them. But then one day somebody I was chatting to told me how discouraged he was because he'd applied to this, that and the other place and had never received a single reply. He said that getting just one reply would have boosted his morale. From then on I always replied to people who wrote to me looking for work, even if it was just to say, 'Sorry, we have no vacancies at the moment.'

* * *

My youngest brother, Joe, made it clear that he didn't want to go into the cafes, but he did say he was very interested in farming. We couldn't see any daylight in this for a while because there didn't seem to be an opening for him. Danum was only a small farm, after all, and Alfred was already looking after that. We decided he should get some experience and he started work on a farm on the northside of Dublin. He lived with the family and worked on their farm. In the early 1940s, when we bought a farm called Knocksedan near Dublin airport, Joe took charge of that. He joined the board of directors in 1949.

My father had been the only MD in his time, but in 1939 Mr Overend and Mr Clark decided at the annual meeting that Alfred and I should both hold the position. Joe joined us at a later stage – in 1960. The three of us used to meet at four o'clock every Monday afternoon in my office to discuss company affairs.

During my father's time staff socials were held some evenings in Westmoreland Street. Also, supper parties were held at Danum for senior members of staff and, in the summer, garden parties were held on the tennis courts for all members of staff. Alfred, Joe and I, with the help and support of our mother, continued these traditions for a number of years. A precedent had been set during my father's time. I felt it was important to continue it and my mother very much backed me in this. As the years went on she became less tied up in her family and she was able to take an interest in a wider circle of things, but she was always all on for encouraging anything that was for the good of mankind, like staff relations in the firm.

Notes

1. Winifred remembers her father and her Uncle Alfred setting off into town on their bicycles. In those days they wore navy suits and white shirts with starched collars.

2. Alfred attended Leeds Bakery College in 1937-8 where he completed a two-year course in one year and gained a first class honours. For many years he was in charge of the Bewley's bakery – a responsibility his son, William, took over some years later.

3. Theodore Halliday joined the firm as a book-keeper and later became general manager of Westmoreland Street. Elizabeth Cassidy was a manageress in Westmoreland Street while Isa Hewson had long been Ernest's private secretary before becoming company secretary. Elizabeth Ward was manageress of Grafton Street shop.

4. When I asked Victor to name some memorable famous customers, he could not answer. His Quaker belief that people are all equal before God prevented him from seeing people as famous or otherwise.

5. Other writers who frequented the cafes include James Joyce, Patrick Kavanagh, Anthony Cronin and Brendan Behan.

6. It wasn't until almost the middle of the century that the trustees of Ernest Bewley's estate were able to pay off the last of the debt incurred by the purchase and refurbishment of Grafton Street. The shares were distributed to his three sons, Victor, Alfred and Joe, and the café leases to his two daughters, Sylvia Poynton and Doris Johnson.

SIX

THE WAR YEARS

When I took over the business I decided to start extending the food on offer beyond sausages and eggs so that people could eat a meal if they wished. We never set out to become a high class restaurant however. It was a gradual process which accelerated during the war years when there were difficulties getting supplies. One of the difficulties for customers was getting enough gas to cook meals at home – they found that one way they could get around this problem was by eating in the cafes. Up until the war we had used gas to fire the ovens. With the rationing of gas, however, we had to find an alternative. We bought stoves which used a variety of fuels and we started to cut turf up on the featherbeds in the Dublin mountains.[1]

The largest amount we ever cut in a year was 300 tonnes. Alfred was in charge of this. The men who cut the turf went up the mountains in a horse and cart, which they used to deliver the fuel to the cafes. The turf was brought straight to the cafes after it had been cut. It wasn't properly dry then and it had to be dried before we could put it into the stoves to burn. It was difficult to dry such large quantities and we used to spread it out on top of the ranges. This process went on all day every day and I remember at one stage spending almost an entire three weeks in the kitchen stoking the old ranges, trying to get the heat up to boil the kettles.

★ ★ ★

At one stage importation of coffee was completely cut off and we couldn't import any at all. I'd been building up stocks, however, and we had about eighteen months supply in hand when it became impossible to ship in any more. Although there was a gap in imports, we never ran out. But we did have to introduce a rationing system for the good coffees: we gave cards to our regular customers and they had to produce them in order to get served.

We also started to make a blend using roast barley. Roast barley is a negative kind of thing, but it blended in reasonably well with coffee. It was all right to use in wartime, but normally we wouldn't want to have used it. During the war years we sold a lot of this coffee and barley blend.

At one stage various firms who were interested in importing coffee got together and, with government assistance, chartered a ship to bring coffee in from the west coast of Africa. That was the only coffee we could get at first: we couldn't get the good coffees, but we were thankful to get any kind of coffee. For some years we continued to import coffee from Angola and neighbouring countries. Tea was rationed to half an ounce per week and a lot of people who had never drunk coffee before started to drink it. We were fortunate in that way: although we were hit because tea was rationed, at least we had another line to offer. Flour was also rationed during the war and, of course, this affected our bakery. We couldn't make a lot of the usual lines, so we started to make things that needed little or no flour, such as oatcakes, oatmeal crunchies and meringues. We were able to make as much as the public wanted of these items. We were short of cream, too, but we started to produce a custard cream substitute to use in our small cakes.

So we were not without challenges during the war years, but we were fortunate in that there were other things we could turn to. Otherwise, we would have been very awkwardly placed.

★ ★ ★

There was great poverty in Dublin during the war years. There had been already, but the war certainly didn't help. Housing conditions were appalling and the slums were dreadful. I remember visiting some families and it was only dreadful the number of people I saw living in one room. Often there was only one toilet in the basement of a whole house full of people.

A hospital doctor, Dr Collis, unearthed a widespread problem through his work. He found that there was nothing wrong with many of the children coming to hospital except that they didn't have a proper diet. They simply weren't getting enough to eat and in hospital they were being given medicines when all they needed was proper food. This situation received a lot of publicity in the papers. It dawned on me one day that here were people who couldn't cook meals because they didn't have any fuel and, yet, we had these ranges in the cafes that were hot all day and could easily be kept hot a little longer in the evening. I realised that if some arrangement could be made to cook meals for these children, then their health would improve. I got in touch with Dr Collis and told him that we would be interested in doing something to help the hungry children. I told him that if somebody could pay for the food that we would do the work voluntarily: there would be no charge for premises, heat or anything else if somebody else could foot the bill for the food.

When it became known in the firm that we were going to do this and that we would need voluntary help after work hours, the vast majority of the staff offered to help. We had an enormous number of volunteers – some offering to stay on after work once a week, others once a fortnight. That is how we came to serve dinners to poor children during the emergency. The kitchen staff put on the stew to cook during the day, but otherwise they didn't do any more work during working hours. Then when we shut at six o'clock the stew was ready for the children who were already queuing up outside, waiting to come in.

The almoners, I suppose they would be called social workers now, in the hospitals sent us lists of names of children who needed feeding. Each child got a plate of stew followed by rice pudding with some jam on top and a mug of milk. We continued providing these meals for three or four years.[2] When the war was over there was still a need to continue for a while and St John's Ambulance took over the responsibility. Eventually – when there was no longer any need – it was discontinued.

* * *

Over the years we donated leftovers at the end of the day's trading to different charities. One of the earliest to receive them was the Little Sisters of the Poor in Kilmainham who looked after elderly people. Their rules were very strict in those days and the nuns used to come to the cafes at the end of the day in a horse-drawn cab that had a little window high up on the side so that they could see out, but nobody could see in. They liked to maintain their privacy, but they came every day and the left-over food was put in bags and given to them.

In the 1960s we gave milk and buns to a school for Travellers on a halting site in Cherry Orchard in Ballyfermot. I forget what other charities we gave leftovers to.

* * *

After the war we had a sudden burst of spending on labour-saving equipment which made us more efficient. We couldn't afford to spend any money before then because we had experienced lean years coming up to the war and we simply hadn't had the money to buy new equipment.

Until the war was over the coffee was made in big seven-pound jam jars in the kitchens and was sent, one jar at a time, up to the cafes in a lift that had to be pulled by hand. There it was poured into urns where it was kept hot. The tea was also made in the kitchens. I can see the girls now: they would carry a tray of teapots over to one of the big kettles sitting on the range where they would fill the pots with boiling water before sending them up on the lifts. It was about as primitive as it could be.

The mornings were always quiet in the kitchens because there weren't many customers, but at lunchtime the place would become busy with everyone in all of a rush. When lots of people came into the cafes you had to try and keep a bit ahead, but not too much ahead or the tea and coffee would get cold.

Notes
1. A section of bog near Glencree is still known as the Bewley Bog.
2. At Christmas Alfred Bewley would dress up as Santa Claus and give presents to the children. Unlike Victor, Alfred was an extrovert and he became known as something of a 'joker' both inside and outside the extended family.

SEVEN

THE BEWLEY
COMMUNITY

The Bewley Community Ltd was a trust set up in 1972 to allow long-term members of staff to participate in the running of the business and to benefit from the firm's profits. Alfred, Joe and I had been thinking about setting it up for a long time because we had always felt that good relationships between staff and management were important. In many different ways we did get the opinions of staff on different things, but there was no formal structure for that to happen and I'm sure a lot of people probably felt that it didn't happen.

It was after I took over the running of the business that I began to develop a great interest in people and in their development. That probably had a lot to do with the reason behind the Community. I felt it was wrong that the staff should have no means of expressing their views and that they should be treated as children in this way. I felt strongly that the staff should have some say in the business. So often you hear of firms that are in trouble having to make changes and how the changes often result in a strike. More than half the time the reason for the trouble is the way the staff are being treated. Often I think staff would accept changes to save their jobs, but their problem is that they can't trust the management.

I thought it was important that people in Bewley's should be treated as though they were fit to have an opinion. The fact that they're allowed to express their point of view and are seen as worthy of expressing it is something very valuable. I've seen people grow in dignity and stature once they have had that opportunity; it really did something for them.

I think if you'd asked my nephews[1] after they joined the firm if they felt they were involved in decision-making they would probably have said no, that the old fellows ran it all. It struck me that if they felt that way, then how on earth must the staff, who have no link with us other than doing their work, feel? It was clear that a further step was needed to translate goodwill into action.

We'd been thinking along those lines for some time when I heard of a firm in Northamptonshire called Scott Barder Commonwealth who had done something that sounded very like what we wanted to do. They produce polyester resin and they are still going strong. I went to visit them and I attended a number of conferences that helped our own ideas to grow and develop. As far as I knew, this was the first time anything like this had been done in Ireland. Other people may have done different things that they felt were appropriate to their situation and we've always said that we didn't feel there was one way for everybody, but that there were probably many different solutions.

Quite often after we made the change, people came to see me and asked why we had done it as they were very interested in doing something similar. But when it came to actually parting with the ownership of the shares, they often couldn't cross that bridge and we didn't usually hear from them again.

Before the Community was set up the shares were mainly held by the family – my two brothers and myself – and by a few senior members of staff. I was still in school when my father had made the firm into a limited company, Bewley's Oriental Cafes Ltd, so that there would be a framework in place for the business carrying on in the event of his death.

In 1972 we changed it from a limited company into a guaranteed company called The Bewley Community Ltd. The shares were held in trust and the members of the Community, who became the owners of the shares, could never gain personally from them. No one could ever be tempted to sell the firm for private gain.

Membership of the Community was open to anyone who had been on the staff for a period of at least three years.

We held a meeting one evening to inform the staff about the Community before it was put in place. They didn't know what it was about beforehand and, afterwards, one man said to me that he had been terrified, when he had seen the notice about the meeting, that we were going to say that the company was going to close. It just shows how people's minds work when they don't know what is going on in a firm. I think most of the staff didn't really understand at first what the Community was all about, but once they knew we weren't going to close they didn't seem to mind what we did.

* * *

The Community was a profit-sharing scheme, although a lot of people thought that, in a way, that was the least important part of it. They felt that the really important part was the control of the ownership of the shares and the opportunity it gave to staff to contribute their ideas, suggestions and opinions to what was going on in the firm.

The profit-sharing scheme worked on the basis that whatever dividend was paid, an equal amount had to be paid to assist underprivileged people. The Community decided who should benefit. An equal amount was paid in dividend which was divided equally amongst the members of the Community. That was decided by the staff. One possibility would have been to have divided the dividend in relation to the salaries staff were being paid which would have meant that those at the highest end would have got the most. The staff decided, however, that it should be equal irrespective of wage or salary. I believe that was the right decision.

The accounts, of course, became known – what we were making or not making. We never made large profits, but I don't think anyone ever realised that until they heard what the profits actually were. We got rid of the bogey that somebody was making large profits at the expense of others because, with the Community, we were all making the same. We made a profit every year bar two in my time, but it was never great and therefore what was divided was never great. The quality of service offered was always given priority over the amount of money made.

The Community had a committee which was elected from different parts of the firm. Each department had one representative bar a couple of very large departments which had two representatives. This produced a committee of twelve and it was this committee that decided which charities should benefit although any members of staff could make a suggestion as to where the money should go. It wasn't possible to cover everybody's suggestions, but we did as many as we could.

We supported all sorts of projects in Dublin. I remember we heard about a youth club that met in a premises where the floor was in very poor condition. They did not have the money to put in a new floor, so we did it for them.

The causes which benefited were not only Irish ones, however. One year somebody suggested supporting a co-operative in Africa which was producing nuts and vegetables. They had tried to store their produce, but it had all been eaten by monkeys. The proposal was that we would provide an up-to-date storage facility so that when they were harvesting they could store their produce and sell it on the market when the price was right.

* * *

I don't remember anything that would have been detrimental to the firm being pushed for, but I do remember one time in the early 1970s that management came under criticism.

There used to be two bakeries – one in Westmoreland Street and one in Grafton Street – and we decided it would be a good idea to combine the two because we were duplicating work. Three of my nephews, Patrick, John and Richard, found premises right in the city centre that they thought would be suitable.

We called a meeting of the bakers to tell them of this proposed acquisition of premises, but they were very unhappy with the suggestion and unanimously opposed it. So we had to drop that idea. Patrick, John and Richard kept searching until they found premises on Long Lane, opposite the Meath Hospital. Another meeting of the bakers was called and this proposal was discussed and unanimously agreed upon. Our two bakeries were combined and everybody was satisfied.

In a way, one of the most important things was the formation of the Council. This consisted of the head of each department and an elected member of each department, with the two larger departments having two elected members. This produced a body of about forty-five people, giving a good representation of people right through the firm. The Council met monthly and, before each meeting, a notice and a copy of the agenda were pinned on the noticeboard in each department. Afterwards a report on the meeting was put up on the wall so that everybody could read it and know what was going on. I'm quite sure everyone didn't read it, but a lot of people did or, at least, they read the bits that affected them. This helped to get rid of the feeling that secrets were being discussed behind closed doors and it served as an outlet for any frustrations or misunderstandings. For instance, when we were changing over from waitress service to self-service a lot of the staff were not in favour of self-service. They would rather have kept the waitress service and it gave an outlet for that matter to be discussed. People could say whatever they wanted, whereas if it had just been introduced without any discussion or any opportunity for people to object I think it would have made the plan very difficult to implement. It was a good way to get rid of that kind of objection.

There was obviously the possibility that the staff might reach a decision we strongly disagreed with, but it was a step we had to take in faith. We believed that, in the right spirit, difficulties could be overcome with understanding.

In the mid-1970s we had a shop in Stillorgan Shopping Centre, but we had no café there[3] and a site went up for sale. The board met and decided it would be a suitable place to set up a café. It seemed like a good opportunity, but we had a problem: if it became known that we were interested in acquiring the premises the price would go up and we'd end up paying far more than we wanted to pay for it. We wondered how this decision could be made democratically. If we were to ask the Council to make the decision it would involve telling over forty people. But how would forty people manage to keep it a secret? So we told the Community committee of twelve people about the situation and asked if they agreed to us pursuing the property and buying it, without informing the rest of the Community. They decided that we should. So the rest of the staff didn't know anything about it until it was all over and we had, in fact, bought the site. Immediately we bought it we held a meeting to which we invited all members of the Council. We told them the position and they decided unanimously that we had done the right thing.

I never harboured any fears of the business slipping out of my control. I had a lot of trust in the staff and so did my brothers. The alternative was to go along the traditional path of managing the firm without consultation, but there would have been things to fear along that road as well.

There were, of course, difficulties to be faced ahead by giving so much power and consultation to the staff, but there were even greater difficulties to be faced in not doing so. Management can be locked in conflict with staff in all kinds of ways as the result of a lack of consultation. So both roads had their problems ahead. You see it on the news and in the papers that this, that or the other firm is threatened with a strike because the management want to implement changes that the staff won't agree to implement. They appear to be threatening their own jobs, but often in these cases I think that, with proper handling, the situation could be resolved before it reaches the conflict stage. So much conflict in the world comes from that kind of situation and people take great risks in time of war for what they believe to be right. Why shouldn't we take some risks for peace in building the kind of world in which we would like to live: a world of co-operation and of respect for people? People respond to being respected.

* * *

People's reactions to the formation of The Bewley Community varied from those who didn't understand and asked, 'Why on earth are you doing this?' to those who felt it was unnecessary and others who felt that it was unwise. Many people said that it would never work; some said they hoped it wouldn't work because, if it did, they might then feel threatened in their own positions. I was always interested in other people's experiences and ideas, but it didn't worry me if people thought we were crackers. They were entitled to think we were crackers. Maybe we were! At the end of the day I believe the Community worked. Oh yes! I do believe it worked.

Notes
1. His nephews were Alfred's sons, Richard and William, Joe's sons, Patrick, Michael and Roger, and John Poynton, eldest son of Victor's sister, Sylvia.
2. The word 'Oriental' was taken out of the name because oriental vases and ornaments had not been sold in Bewley's since the Second World War.
3. The Bewley's shop in Stillorgan Shopping Centre opened on 13th May 1970 and the café followed several years later. The shop and café in Dundrum Shopping Centre opened on 13th December 1971. The idea of moving into the suburbs came from the younger generation: Victor, Alfred and Joe were not particularly keen on the idea. John Poynton, who joined the firm in 1952 on a wage of £6 a week, remembers that they agreed to go along with it, lending their help and support along the way.

EIGHT

BUSINESS AS USUAL

In the early hours of the morning on 9th March 1977 I received a phone call from an *Irish Times* reporter. He was looking for a comment on what had happened to Bewley's. I didn't know what he was talking about, but as soon as he rang off Patrick Bewley was on the phone telling me that the Westmoreland Street premises was on fire.[1] He said that he and John Poynton were already on the scene and that the fire brigade was fighting to bring the blaze under control.[2]

I didn't go into town until the normal opening time because I was satisfied that the situation was under control. There was nothing I could have done anyhow. So I went in at my usual time of nine o'clock to start the process of re-building the business. I found that none of the rooms had been left untouched by the fire, although some were worse than others. The coffee shop was largely gutted, as was the cake shop. My office was completely gutted and all my letters and records were gone. I just thought to myself, 'Where do I begin?' But I found that, once I started doing something constructive, I began to feel better.

A little incident in the afternoon helped too. It was my normal practice each day to walk from Westmoreland Street, where I was based, to the cafes on Grafton Street and South Great Georges Street. I did that as usual that day, but I had no coat with me because my gaberdine had been hanging in my office and it had been destroyed in the fire. On the way back from my walk, I called into a man's clothes shop, Kennedy & McSharry's, where I bought a new coat. That was a positive step. And it made me feel better.

The next door shop on Westmoreland Street was empty at the time: we got the use of it and we opened a shop there the next day. So we were only shut completely for one day. The staff were terrific and the maintenance men worked right through the night to get the vacant premises ready to open the following day. It was another five days before we could open the 'smoke room' at the back of the cake shop. And it was another two years and three months before we could re-open the café.

* * *

While we never made big profits, Bewley's was still profitable when I retired at the end of 1977. On my retirement my brothers, Alfred and Joe, retired as managing directors. They continued to work as directors however.

We thought it would be a good idea to have the younger generation in a position of leadership. I suggested to the board that I would have a private conversation with each member of the board – that was roughly a dozen people – and ask them who they would like as managing director when I left.

Apart from Alfred, Joe and myself, the other family members on the board at that time were my daughter, Rachel Bewley, and my nephews, John Poynton and Richard, William, Patrick and Roger Bewley. The rest of the board consisted of Brendan Mealy, Herbert Scott, Beatrice Lunney and John Thompson.

As a result of these conversations, it was decided to appoint John Poynton, Richard Bewley and Patrick Bewley. I was happy with the board's decision. Richard, in fact, emigrated to America the following year[3] which left Patrick and John as managing directors. In 1985 John left the firm to set up a franchise shop in Blackrock, leaving Patrick as the sole managing director and the only family member left in the business.

I know there are some people who blame the setting up of the Bewley Community for the change leading to the situation where the firm had to be sold in 1986. I would not accept that. The 1980s was a time of difficulty for many firms and Bewley's was not the only one to encounter difficulties. In my opinion, the firm's difficulties did not stem from the changes made by my brothers and myself.

In 1986 the Community made the decision to sell the firm to Campbell Catering.[4] They had great difficulty in making the decision, but under the circumstances there was nothing else they could have done. I was glad the firm was going to continue, but I was sorry that the experiment with the Community was not. It was something I had looked forward to and which I had planned for a long time before it came about in 1972. I felt that a lot of my life's work had gone into it, but at this stage there is nothing I can do about it. It is just one of those things I have to accept.

* * *

I was forty-four years as Managing Director of Bewley's Cafes and, for a long time, I resented being there. Throughout the whole of my life I felt I was not cut out to be in business. However, although I knew it wasn't the kind of thing I was cut out for, I accepted I had to do it. And I got on with it. I got a great deal of interest and enjoyment out of it as well as a lot of headaches. Looking back on it now, I don't resent it anymore, thank goodness. I wouldn't like to be resentful in my old age.

Notes
1. I remember Victor rang our house early that morning, about 6.30am, to tell us about the fire before we would hear it on the news. Being the only one up at the time, I answered the phone. I was puzzled that he asked straightaway to speak to my mother, without wanting to chat to me. He sounded quite shaken.
2. The cause of the fire was never discovered. It is thought it may have been the result of an electrical fault or the work of vandals. Firemen, some reportedly in tears at the sight of one of Dublin's oldest cafes going up in flames, worked through the night in an attempt to save the building.
3. Richard, who had joined the firm in 1959, moved with his family to West Chester where his wife, Jo, originally came from. He became director of a retirement community and Jo set up a business in 1982 importing Bewley's teas and other Irish products to the US.
4. Campbell Catering Ltd was established in 1967 by Patrick Campbell. Patrick Bewley stayed on under the new management and in 1988 he became managing director of a new subsidiary called Bewleys Ltd, which is responsible for tea, coffee and the bakery. He has since become its chairman.

VOLUNTARY
WORK

NINE

TRAVELLING PEOPLE

I can remember, when I was a boy, seeing Travellers camped across the river from our farm. They used to camp on the big open space beside the big archway on Dodder Road Lower. It wasn't our land: the farm went down as far as the river and they were camped on the far side. They used to send their horses across the river to graze on our land, though, which didn't please my father. He wasn't the least bit interested in the Travellers.

I, however, was fascinated by their brightly painted caravans, their clutter of children and their horses, dogs, hens and bantams. They looked altogether very interesting and I used to dream about going to visit them. I wanted to get to know such interesting people: their lives seemed so uncomplicated, carefree and picturesque.

My next encounter with a group of Travellers came years later, when I was in my thirties and I was on holiday in Kerry. I was walking across the Connor Pass, from Dingle to Castlegregory, when I saw this group of people ahead of me camped at the side of the road. They had a small brown tent and smoke was drifting up their fire. I remember wondering to myself who they were and what they were like.

As I walked past their camp one of the men, who had been standing on his own, passed the time of day. I responded, but I never slackened my pace: I just kept on walking. But I had the feeling that if I'd stopped to chat he'd have been quite prepared to get into conversation.

I realised there had been something in me that was hesitant about getting into conversation with the man. This surprised me because here were the people I'd been so interested in many years ago and, now that I had the chance to talk to them, I didn't want to take it. I was withdrawn. Why didn't I stop? Was he not one of the people that had so fascinated me in earlier life? What had happened since? Two things, perhaps. There was nothing picturesque or romantic about this man and his simple camp. On the contrary, he was quite shabby and downtrodden in his appearance, with rather a hopeless expression on his face. Secondly, for my part, I had been conditioned by all that had happened since childhood. Perhaps, too, I had a feeling that he was going to ask me for something and that, if I had given him something, he would have asked for more. Without realising it, a barrier had arisen between Travellers and myself. I was a member of the settled community and these people were somehow outside and apart and to be regarded with reserve, if not suspicion. And I realised how prejudice and fear of the unknown can condition one.

I knew about the prejudices Travellers faced in those days and I realised that it was in me, just as it was in many other people. That helped me a little bit in understanding other people's prejudices. I thought of the words of Jesus when he said, 'Unless you change and become like little children, you will never enter the kingdom of heaven' (Matthew 18:3). I thought what a pity it was that as we grow up we often lose the open mind of a child who simply sees another human being, unfettered by fears and prejudices which may warp our lives and cloud our vision in later years, thus losing that spirit which helps us to see other people as brothers and sisters in Christ.

★ ★ ★

Travellers were traditionally rural people: they didn't normally live in towns and they didn't want to. They travelled around doing their own business of making and mending pots and pans and making tin mugs, milk cans, buckets and so on. They also used to clean chimneys and deal in horses.

During the 1950s, however, these ways of making a living began to disappear. Plastic began to take the place of old tin utensils and tractors and other machinery began to replace the work previously done by Travellers with their horses. For this reason, Travellers were forced to move to urban areas in order to make a living, largely in those days supported by begging. But they were only begging because their way of livelihood had gone and they had no alternative.

They knew that if they settled and had their children educated, the door would open to other opportunities. It proved difficult for them to settle however: as a result of fear and prejudice, members of the settled community objected to Travellers living near them.

In 1960 the government appointed a committee, the Commission on Itinerancy, to look into the issue. Its findings, published three years later, indicated that of the 1,100 traveller families living in Ireland at that time, 900 families wanted to settle. It was a very good report and I read it with great interest: it was practical, very human and very Christian.

The committee recommended the provision of serviced halting sites and that Travellers be allowed to settle down and live in dignity. Its plans were held up, however, because of prejudice.

I wasn't involved in the committee. I didn't know anything about Travellers at that time and I didn't particularly want to become involved. But around the time of the publication of the report there was a lot of publicity given to the issue and I used to read the press reports with interest.

I drove into work every day through Inchicore and there had been a group of families camped there by the side of the road for a while. One day, while I was passing, I saw all their caravans lined up at the side of the road. The Gardaí were there and it was obvious that the Travellers were being moved on. I thought to myself what a terrible thing it was that in their own country – after all, they were Irish people who didn't have homes anywhere else – they were being evicted lock, stock and barrel with nowhere to go. I knew that wherever they went, the same thing would probably happen to them. These thoughts were going around in my head, making me feel guilty. I felt that something should be done. But it never occurred to me that I should be the one to do it. After all, I knew nothing about Travellers.

* * *

At around this time another Dublin Quaker, Brenda Yasin, became interested in Travellers and she brought up the subject at Friends' Dublin Monthly Meeting (see Appendix). She began to collect funds to start a school on a site at Cherry Orchard in Ballyfermot.

In 1964 Monthly Meeting received a letter asking us to help keep the Cherry Orchard site open. As a result of this letter, my brother, Alfred, and I went to visit the site. There were forty-three families living there at the time and the conditions were simply dreadful. Some of the families were living in huts made out of old packing cases. Yet, in the middle of all the mud and the scrap, I remember there was a little shrine made of white stones and flowers. And I thought to myself what wonderful evidence that was of the spirit of man reaching out to higher things.

While Alfred and I were inside one of the huts, chatting to a family, a woman suddenly appeared, followed by a priest. I recognised the woman to be Lady Eleanor Wicklow – we had met before – but I didn't know the priest. He turned out to be Fr Fehily – Monsignor Fehily, as he is now.[1] Lady Wicklow and Fr Fehily had come to see the conditions, just as we had. They had a very strong feeling that we had not met by chance: that here was the step forward we were all looking for. I said to Lady Wicklow, 'You know far more people than I do. Will you call a committee to try and get a move on the implementation of the report?' 'You must give me time to think about it,' she replied.

I gave her a week and then I rang her up and asked could she and Fr Fehily meet me in my office to discuss the situation over a cup of coffee. We met the next Monday morning and, for some time, we continued to meet in my office every Monday morning. We decided to appoint a committee to see where we could go from there.

We each invited somebody we thought would be suitable to help and that's how the Dublin Itinerant Settlement Committee came to be formed in early 1965. Our aim was to win the support of public opinion for the provision of halting sites. We later changed the name to the Dublin Committee for Travelling People. Originally, Travellers had been called Tinkers – a name that came from their trade of tinkering with pots and pans. It wasn't a derogatory term, but over time it became derogatory. The government committee officially changed their name to Itinerants – a term that also became derogatory.

We decided to use the term Travelling People – after all, they have always referred to themselves as Travellers. The only reason we hadn't used that name in the first place was because it might have sounded as if we were talking about a committee for commercial travellers.

We began to receive enquiries and letters from people all over the country who were also interested in Travellers and who wanted to see something done. People sent us money, saying, 'Thank goodness, at last somebody is going to do something'. We met everyone who contacted us to hear about what they were doing. Various committees around the country were formed, but they felt quite isolated and asked the Dublin committee to call a meeting and invite members of all the committees to it so that they could work together as a national body, instead of everybody just working in their own isolated corner.

We arranged meetings from time to time that we invited the country committees to and in 1969 we decided to form a national committee

Joshua Bewley, Victor's grandfather,
who founded Bewley's Cafes in the early 1840s

*Ernest Bewley, Victor's father and Director of Bewley's Cafes,
pictured circa 1900*

*Danum, the house in Rathgar, Dublin, where Victor grew up
and which was built by his father in 1900*

Victor, as a baby, pictured at Danum in 1912

Victor and his siblings pictured in 1931.
From left to right: Alfred, Victor, Doris, Sylvia and Joe
(picture courtesy of Doris Johnson)

Victor, aged 19, on a trip up the mountains with his parents,
Ernest and Susan, and his sister, Doris

Victor and Winnie cut the cake, made by Bewley's bakery,
on their wedding day on 9th June 1937

Victor and Winnie pictured outside their Connemara cottage,
Rockstrow, in July 1952

Painting, boat trips and picnics always featured in
family holidays to Connemara.

At home with his three daughters, from left, Winifred, Rachel and Heather

Victor chats to a young Traveller woman on the occasion
of her baby's christening

Fiona Murdoch and her son, Ruari, pictured in August 1999
in the Bentley once owned by Ernest Bewley

Victor Bewley receives an honorary doctorate degree
from the Chancellor of Trinity College Dublin, Dr F.H. Boland,
on 6th July 1976

made up of representatives from all the committees. And so the National Council for Travelling People was formed. I was its Secretary and, later, Chairman. The aim of the original settlement committee was threefold. Firstly, to get suitable accommodation provided for Travellers. Secondly, to provide education for Travellers. And thirdly, to get rid of discrimination. Those were the three main aims and they are still the same now, thirty years later.

I was mainly involved with the issue of accommodation. Settled people used to say to us that Travellers wouldn't want to settle down and that they wouldn't want to live in houses. Well, that wasn't true for all families and we had to remember that it was important to consider the wishes of each family. Some very nice accommodation has been provided, but there is a long way to go yet.

In 1964 the Minister for Local Government, Neil Blaney, asked local authorities throughout the country to provide halting sites for Travellers. By the following year, however, nothing had been done because whenever a site had been proposed people in the neighbourhood had so bitterly opposed it that the project had been abandoned. Our committee met with Dublin County Council officials and they informed us that 12 sites had been proposed, but that all had been turned down because of local opposition. So it became clear that if public sites were to be provided that public opinion must be won in favour of them.

People objected because of their fear and prejudice and a great deal of energy, on my part, was taken up over the years in trying to overcome prejudice. I could, at times, get very mad at certain people who were prejudiced in this way, as I saw the damage it was doing to Travellers.

Following our meeting with council officials, the Bewley firm decided to offer five acres of land on its farm at Ballyowen, Clondalkin. We offered the land to the council, free of charge, for the provision of an official site. This produced an awful storm of protest from the neighbours, which was very hard on Alfred and Mary Bewley who were living on the farm. They got a lot of abuse, but they put up with it which was a great credit to them both. Subsequently, as a result of local objections, the council did not go ahead with a site and the committee decided to apply for planning permission to create a site themselves. Initially the application was turned down because there were so many objections, but we appealed the decision and eventually got permission. The restrictions, however, were so unsatisfactory that the committee could not proceed. The application took three days and it was reported in the press which gave great publicity to the cause. In one way it didn't matter that we couldn't proceed because it was good just to get so much publicity.

There was one family we knew who were living under a canvas tent and said they wanted to settle. They went to live (unofficially) at Ballyowen where they camped for a number of years. The parents stayed there until they got a council house and when the eldest son got married he and his wife took to the road again. They returned when their first baby was on its way and they camped there until they, too, got a council house.

★ ★ ★

As time went on I became terribly anxious that land would be found to somehow get the first campsite going so that people could see that it was a workable alternative. In the summer of 1965 Winnie and I and our youngest daughter Heather, who was still living with us, wondered would we allow some families to come and camp on our land, but we weren't clear in our minds that we felt happy about doing this.

After all, Winnie or Heather could have been in the house for hours on their own during the day. And, anyway, the Travellers looked different and they seemed a bit strange. We didn't know them or who they would bring with them. People said that if we gave permission for one family to camp that we'd have forty the next day. Also, we felt that because of our isolated location twelve miles from Dublin, and being 1,000 foot up in the mountains, it would be too cold and harsh in winter and that it really wouldn't be suitable to invite Travellers to live here. So we decided against the idea and we didn't mention the subject again for another three months.

During that time, however, we began to realise that we were reacting in the same way that everybody else was reacting to Travellers. Because of our own fears and suspicions we didn't want anything to do with them. We went through great heart-searching as we wondered how we could go to meeting for worship on a Sunday morning and think about love and understanding when we knew that we had land where families could live. The only reason we didn't invite any families to live here was because we were afraid to do so.

Again, it came across very clearly that we were reacting in exactly the same way as everybody else. Because of our fear and prejudice we were doing nothing. And we became uneasy with our decision.

Finally, as winter approached, we couldn't tolerate the situation any longer and we decided we would offer land to a traveller family to come and stay. A family soon moved in, but they left after three weeks because it was too lonely for them. They camped beside Connors cottage, a disused dwelling on our land, and I remember the mother of the family saying that if only they were camped on the roadside, where there was traffic passing, they wouldn't feel so isolated and lonely. They had been part of a large group of families and they began to miss the company of their relatives and friends. And so on a dark afternoon as the snow was falling, they left their new home to return to join their relatives on the road.

It was a disappointment to us that they left so soon, but we benefited from the experience. We learnt that there must be at least two families if it was going to be a success. And the heart-searching process beforehand had taught us another important lesson – to understand the prejudice of other people.

Two families came after that and they stayed for a while until they got other accommodation. Another two families came and they stayed for a couple of years. All in all, we had Travellers living here for about four years.

The Hands family probably stayed the longest. They had settled in very quickly: within a few hours, literally, of their arriving the young man started cutting the hedge, making a path and digging flower beds where he soon started to grow vegetables as well as a variety of flowers. At the end of his second day he said to me, 'I cannot understand why the other family left here. My wife and I are so happy, we feel we will never leave here. The place is so homely.' They had the most delightful children – full of friendliness and goodwill. Whenever I went to visit they would come running out and put their little hands in mine, saying, 'Mammy's inside. Are you going to come in?'

When I looked at these children and felt their friendliness and life bubbling over, I felt the terrible wrong that could be done to them if they should feel that their friendliness would be turned away by the settled community. How easy it would be for them to grow up into antagonistic, anti-social adults if they were treated as social outcasts. If that happened it would be our fault, not theirs: they were reaching out the hand of friendship and it was up to us to take it.

Each of the families had the use of one room in the cottage. The Dublin Itinerant Settlement Committee also provided a caravan for each of them for which they paid a nominal rent.

Our own fears and prejudices disappeared while the families were staying here. We had feared that they might invite other families and that the whole thing might get out of hand, but that didn't happen.

I overcame my own initial prejudices by getting to know Travellers and by realising that they were people, just like ourselves. Their children were uppermost in their minds and, in that respect, they were no different from us. I saw how family-orientated they were and how many of them like to live with their extended families, which has a lot of advantages. They take good care of their old people and the families need to be together to do this.

The Travellers as a whole are not a community: their loyalty is to their own family group. These ties are very strong and should be preserved because they have considerable social advantages. When a mother has to go into hospital, there is someone to care for the children if she is living near some of her relatives. And when the parents get old, there is someone at hand to care for them.

I remember one time there was a group of families who had nowhere to go. Among them were two young couples, each with a young baby. It was November and they were camped in very poor tents in Milltown. One day the first couple went to a nearby convent to ask for help, but the baby died on the way in her mother's arms. It was such a shock to the poor mother that she lost her power of speech and she had to go into hospital. This left the father with six children to look after and their only means of support was the children's allowance.

A month later the baby of the second couple died of pneumonia. That evening I was passing through Milltown, near where the Travellers were camped, and I saw a group of them squatting in a corner grieving. They were showing their emotions much more than we would and I am sure that many who saw them passed harsh judgements on them. But few knew the tragedy that lay behind the scene.

If we have a death in the family we tend to keep a stiff upper lip, as though we can cope, whereas Travellers express their feelings far more. Maybe settled people might be better off expressing their feelings more at a time of death, rather than trying to bottle them up, which only produces psychological problems later on.

We make a mistake if we think that all Travellers are dirty or that they are happy to live in squalor. Many of the nuisances we associate with

Travellers arise not from the people themselves, but from the conditions in which they are forced to live. Many of them will change when their conditions change. This has been proved over and over again. Many traveller sites are, of course, dirty and unsanitary. It is impossible for them to be otherwise under the conditions in which the families have to live. No water and no sanitation equals muddy ground. And herein lies the advantage to the settled community of a properly equipped site: it gets rid of this objectionable aspect as well as being of benefit to the Travellers themselves.

I remember visiting one family with Fr Fehily. A heavy polythene sheet covered three mattresses placed one on top of the other. In front of this there was a little windbreak made out of carpets and sacking and corrugated iron and behind this a fire was burning in a bucket. This was the home of a man and his wife and two little boys for the whole of that winter. The place was damp, muddy and dirty and, at night, the rats came and ran around them. And when you're lying on a mattress on the ground, of course, the rats are at very close quarters. After the committee moved the family into a caravan, the woman told us that living in her new home was like 'being out of pain'.

There are, of course, those in the travelling community for whom drink is a problem, just as there are those in the settled community for whom drink is a problem. But this does not mean that this is true for all Travellers or for all of the settled community.

Of course, some Travellers are dishonest just as some settled people are dishonest. We must not judge the majority by the few. When treated reasonably, they are just as well able, and as likely, to co-operate as anyone else. When they are treated as outcasts why should they co-operate or consider the wishes of those who have had so much greater opportunities in life, yet rejected them? I remember meeting one young man whose father had a drink problem and who frequently got into fights. The man had been provided with accommodation by the committee and he was anxious to do his very best to provide for his wife and children.

'Of course, I don't tell the fellows where I'm working that I ever came off the road,' he told me one day.

'Why not?' I said. 'There's nothing wrong with being on the road.'

'Oh yes,' he said. 'But people think that if you have been on the road, then if you see something that you want – even if it's not yours – that you'll take it.'

'Oh yes. I know there are people on the road like that, but we have people like that in the settled community too. Not everyone like that is on the road.'

'Well, you know that, but other people don't. They think we're all the same. If they find out that I came off the road, I'm going to leave my job.'

'Don't you do any such thing,' I told him. 'You stick to your guns and let them see that you are different.'

This young man was going through a terrible struggle: he was fighting against such odds. I thought a terrible crime would have been committed against him if he should be kept back by the stigma wrongly attached to him.

I know there are troublemakers in the travelling community, but that does not mean all Travellers should get a bad name. We are making a dreadful mistake if we think that Travellers are all the same. People say to me that if Travellers did this, that or the other, then they would feel differently about them. But we must remember that Jesus did not wait for people to be perfect to love them. He loved them as they were and, in so doing, helped them and inspired them on to better things.

* * *

One day in early 1974 I had a visit from a young man who worked for the Department of the Environment. Part of his job involved working with Travellers and he said he needed a briefing on the subject. Following our discussion, he told me that there was a few people in government who wanted to meet me to discuss the traveller situation. When I arrived at the meeting I found about a dozen people waiting for me. There were three or four government ministers in the room as well as a number of civil servants representing different departments. We had a good discussion on Travellers and they listened to what I had to say.

I wasn't long back in the office when I got a telephone call to say that Declan Costelloe, who was Attorney General at the time, would like to see me. And that he wanted me to come quickly. So I went that afternoon to see him. He explained that a sort of trap had been laid for me that morning. The meeting had, in fact, been an interview to see if I would be suitable to fill a new position they wished to create – a post of national adviser to the government on the settlement of Travellers. They wanted the programme for Travellers to proceed more quickly and they wanted to know what could be done to achieve that. They needed advice on the matter. They were finding it hard to find someone suitable to fill the position and they wondered if I would take it. They said I could have whatever facilities I would like – an office, a salary and expenses. They were offering me a full-time post if I wanted it, but I didn't want that because we had recently set up the Bewley Community and I didn't want to sever my connections with the firm.

After giving the matter some consideration I put it to them that I couldn't accept a full-time post, but that I could accept a part-time one. And I said that, no thanks, I wouldn't need an office because I could work from the one I already had in Westmoreland Street. They agreed.

I brought this to the board of Bewley's with the suggestion that I would go part-time and that my salary would be docked by the amount I was getting from the government. The board agreed and we told the staff at a Council meeting so that they would know why, in future, I would be unavailable at certain times.

And so in March 1974 James Tully, Minister for Local Government, appointed me as his adviser on the programme for the settlement of travelling people. I was more or less given a free hand. There was nobody to give me instructions or to tell me how to go about the work, so I had to make the job for myself. I decided on a programme of visiting every county to see what the position was and, by the time I had done that, there was no end of problems needing attention. Initially I worked only half a day a week, but I did a lot of work in my spare time, too.

I always got on well with county councils and, on the whole, I found them positive. I always wrote to the manager of a site before going to visit and I realised that the managers hadn't an easy job because they were up against the public. So I never had hard feelings against them. I visited every official site around the country at least once. I also saw many proposed sites. I was often asked to visit these with a committee in order to give my opinion. I was always happy to do this. I didn't visit every proposed site, though – the ones I tended to visit were either of a new design or ones where there were difficulties.

There was always plenty to be done and I was glad to be able to give more time to it after I retired from Bewley's in 1977. I came into my office two or three days a week to continue my work with Travellers.

Pádraig Flynn was Minister for the Environment and Local Government when in 1988 I decided it was time to retire from my advisory post. He told me that I could retire so long as I told him of a suitable person to take my place. I suggested to him Fr Christy Jones –

now Bishop Jones of Sligo. He was a good deal younger than I was and he had been interested in Travellers for many years. And so Fr Jones was duly appointed.

* * *

In July 1976 I was awarded an honorary degree from Trinity College Dublin. I had great hesitation in receiving it: I remember when I got the letter I didn't reply for a long time because I don't hold with that sort of thing.[2] I'd already refused another couple of awards because I don't believe in picking out one person over another. There were many wonderful people I met over the years in my work with Travellers whose names will never be known.[3]

An increasing number of Travellers have gone through education now, albeit in varying amounts. Some have had more or less full-time education while others have had only partial education. Education opens doors to Travellers, allowing them to take up jobs previously denied to them because they couldn't read or write. Some are now becoming teachers and taking up other good jobs. There is a traveller on Galway County Council who is not there as a representative of Travellers, but was voted on by everybody – settled people and Travellers alike. That is visible progress.

A lot has happened, but a lot more has got to happen. Getting rid of discrimination has always been the most difficult aim. In some ways, there is worse prejudice today than there used to be, but on the other hand a lot of progress has been made. The settled community has a better understanding of Travellers now.

Another bit of progress is that county councils throughout the country are much more open to understanding the different ways of Travellers. This has come about by experience and by realising that mistakes have been made. For example, there is no point in providing a site in an unsuitable location because it simply won't work.

There are now over 3,000 families who have been provided with some kind of accommodation, but there are still over 1,000 families on the roadside with no accommodation.[4]

Some Travellers would like to be housed and some would like to be in a group housing scheme where a group of related families can live together. Some don't want a house, but would like to live on a halting site with water and sanitation and a hard surface where they can park their caravans. They suffer badly in the winter with the muck the ground gets into when there is no hard surface.

After all this time – it is more than thirty years now since the publication of the government report – people wonder why there is still the same number of families on the road. The reason, of course, is that the total number of families has increased during that period.

Travellers are speaking for themselves more and more now and this is very much to be encouraged. They are a very interesting people and I think it would be a great pity if, in a couple of generations, they became completely integrated into the settled community.

Notes

1. Monsignor Fehily is Parish Priest of St Michael, Dún Laoghaire.
2. Winifred says her father finally agreed to accept the honorary degree on the understanding that he was accepting it on behalf of all those who worked towards improving conditions for Travellers. Some of these people were among his guests at the ceremony. He also hoped the award would help to highlight the issue. Recipients are normally expected to wear 'dress suit' for the occasion, but the authorities gave Victor special dispensation to wear his customary tweed suit on the grounds of his Quaker belief in simplicity of dress and lifestyle.
3. Apart from the Most Rev Jones and Monsignor Fehily, the following were also closely involved with Victor in his work with Travellers – Sr Colette Dwyer, Sr Robartz, Joyce Sholdice, Vincent Jones and Victor Foley. Sheila Pim, a Quaker who lived in Bray, invited Traveller families to live on her land and she also set up a school for Traveller children in her home.
4. According to the Irish Traveller Movement, figures for 2001 show that there are now more than 5,000 Traveller families living in Ireland. Of these, 1,018 are living on the side of the road with no services and 1,192 are on halting sites while 456 are accommodated in group housing schemes and 2,272 in council houses.

TEN

CROSS-BORDER TALKS

In February 1972 I received in the post a pamphlet called *The Burden of Northern Ireland*. It was terribly bitter and anti the Republic or anything to do with the South. There was no letter with it and there was no name on it: it just said in the introduction that it was compiled and distributed by 'a group of moderate Protestants/Unionists'.

It was a duplicated pamphlet, so I knew it hadn't just been sent to me. Why it was sent to me, I don't know. I felt very strongly that I would like to reply to whoever sent it, but I couldn't because there was no name or address on it. I decided, instead, to write to the three morning papers – *The Irish Times*, *The Irish Independent* and *The Irish Press* – in the hopes that the person who wrote the letter would see it. I wrote the same letter to each of the papers. The theme of the letter was that, although we were different groups of people living on this island, what we had in common was far greater than what divided us in religious matters. I explained why I was writing the letter to the press: I couldn't reply to the letter I had received in any other way. My letter to the papers resulted in a host of replies, about sixty or seventy, mostly from people in the North. They were mainly favourable, agreeing with the sentiments I had expressed. But a few were very bitter and critical.

A number of the letters were from very genuine and sincere people who were frustrated because they felt there was nothing that they could do about the situation. I thought it was a pity to leave all that goodwill there and I thought somebody should hold onto that kind of spirit. So I decided to call a meeting and invite all those who had replied to me. I got the use of the lecture room in the Friends' Meeting House at Eustace Street, Dublin. About sixty people turned up. I told them about what had happened – about all the letters I had received and about the amount of goodwill that was out there. And I told them that the purpose of the meeting was to promote understanding and that it was an opportunity to enlarge what was in people's minds. There was no attempt to reach any decision or conclusion or anything like that. What we wanted to work towards was an understanding.

At the end of the meeting a man came up to me and said he was in business in Dublin and that a few of his friends, most of whom were also in business, had been meeting regularly to see what could be done about reconciliation in the north. He said that they would like me to become chairman of their group. I said I couldn't possibly become their chairman because I didn't know anything about their group or what they were trying to do, but I told him I would be pleased to go to one of their meetings.

It turned out to be quite a good group. Two members came to see me one day in my office and said they would like me to meet another group they were involved with. They were Catholics and they had a number of contacts with the Irish Republican Army in Dublin whom they were anxious I should meet as soon as possible. I wasn't in a hurry to do this because I knew that various people were meeting IRA leaders at that time and I felt that this was filling the IRA with their own importance. So I was reluctant to go and meet any of them.

Finally, however, I did agree to meet some of them; I met different ones at different places. The first time was on a Saturday afternoon and I was to meet Seán MacStiofáin who was one of the high up men in the IRA at that time. Four or five of us went to meet him. There was another Quaker, an Englishman called Walter Martin, and the others were from the Catholic businessmen's group.

I remember we crossed Phoenix Park to a line of houses on the other side. We were to meet Seán MacStiofáin in one of those houses, but the crowd that were bringing us didn't seem to know which house which made it a bit difficult! Finally, they decided which house it was and we knocked on the door. A lady answered and asked us who we wanted to see. She ushered us into a room where we waited. She didn't seem to know who we were or why we were there.

Finally, the other crowd arrived – Seán MacStiofáin and two or three others. So it turned out we were in the right house after all. We all had tea and cakes and chat. I think he was arrested shortly after that.

There was another meeting one Saturday evening at a house near the RDS showgrounds. Again, it was at the invitation of the Catholic businessmen's group. This time we were going to meet Daithí Ó Conaill who, at that time, was the top man in the IRA. This meeting followed much the same procedure as before. We met in a pavilion at the end of somebody's garden – it was full of sports equipment and gardening tools. We just had a general chat; there was no definite outcome from the meeting.

* * *

Sometime after that, Winnie and I were sitting by the fire one Sunday evening when the telephone rang and it was one of the men from the businessmen's group. 'I want to bring a friend of mine to see you,' he said, 'And I'd like to do it this evening.' 'That's all right. Come along,' I replied.

It wasn't until I put the phone down that I realised I hadn't asked who was coming to see me. In due course the doorbell rang and I went to answer the door. There were two men outside whom I didn't know. The man who had rung me hadn't come with them, but that didn't matter.
I remember one man was standing back in the dark and the other was standing under the light. When I was friendly towards them and invited them to come in the man who was barely visible stepped forward into the light. I think he wanted to see what my reaction would be. It was, in fact, Daithi Ó Conaill. The other fellow was a reporter from one of the daily papers.

When they came inside Daithi Ó Conaill started off by asking me if I had any contacts in the British government. 'No, I haven't,' I said. 'But I can make contact if you want me to. Why do you ask?' 'Will you take an offer of peace from the IRA to the British government?' he asked. 'I will if you tell me what you want me to say,' I replied. 'Will you please write down your message because if I'm talking to somebody in the British government I want to make sure I pass on the message accurately?'

I gave him a piece of paper and a pen and he wrote down three points. I still have the piece of paper he wrote on.

I phoned London to speak to Walter Martin. At that time he was secretary of Friends Service Council[1] and he had contacts with many different groups all over the world. Unfortunately he was going into hospital to have an operation, but I took a flight to England a few days later anyway. Walter had arranged for me to meet up with another Quaker.

The two of us went to see someone at government buildings in Westminster, but unfortunately it was not somebody high enough for what we wanted. I asked him if he would come to Ireland and meet some Republicans without any commitment. But he quite obviously would have been terrified to do so. In fact, he would not do so under any circumstances. We talked about this backwards and forwards for a while. I told him that if he came I would put him up in my home and that I would accompany him from the time he stepped off the aeroplane until the time he got on it again to go home. But there was no way he would come. So that was that.

I had hoped that some kind of ongoing discussion might come out of it, but one of the IRA's conditions was the complete withdrawal of the British troops from the North by a certain date. That used to come up with the same regularity as talk of decommissioning arms comes up at the present.

I returned to Ireland and the arrangement had been that I would contact the reporter and that he would contact Daithí Ó Conaill to arrange a meeting. A short while after that there was a ring on the doorbell one Sunday evening and this time Daithí Ó Conaill had come on his own. We had a long chat and it was a very good chat.

All these people tend to be watched by their colleagues and it makes them very cagey about what they'll say in front of somebody else, so it was great having nobody else there because it meant we could talk frankly. 'Will you go back to London again and see if you can get them to come over?' Daithí asked me. He was very anxious to have a cessation of violence. I said that I would go again.

That was on a Sunday and I was to go two days later, on the Tuesday. But on the Monday I had a visit from the reporter with a message from Daithí to tell me not to go because the Northern Irish element of the IRA were much more hard-line than those in the South and it was no longer appropriate for me to go. So I didn't go.

A short while after that he came to see me in my office. This was after I had retired and I still had an office at 19/20 Fleet Street, which meant that people coming to see me could come in through a side door and up the stairs. Virtually nobody could see them and anybody could have come in. Daithí came to see me there several times.[2] He gave me his telephone number so that if I wanted to speak to him anytime I could phone him – I did on a number of occasions. Unfortunately, he died suddenly and that was the end of that contact.

I did meet other members of the IRA who were older than Daithí – he was probably one of the younger members. One night a young man from the group brought two well-known republicans – John Kelly, who was just out of jail, and Joe Cahill – to see me at my house. It was always on a Sunday evening, for some reason.

* * *

I kept in touch with the English Quaker, Walter Martin, over a long period of time. He was anxious that we should meet some Loyalists. I don't think he had anybody in particular in mind, but he arranged with me that the two of us should meet in Belfast on Thursday of Holy Week. It was of no particular significance that it was Holy Thursday – it was just that we were both free that day.

It was snowing and the ground was white. Walter had arrived in the North before me and he had rung up the offices of one of the Loyalist organisations and asked could he speak to somebody. He identified himself and fixed an appointment.

He met me at the train station and we got a taxi and went to a particular address he had been told to go to. The person we met there was obviously somebody important in the movement. It wasn't a very large room, but he was at a desk at one end that had three or four telephones sitting on it. He was sitting there answering any calls that came in.

We were sitting facing him and behind us there was a fellow on a ladder painting the ceiling. I thought it was rather odd to have somebody painting the ceiling during a meeting. We were not alone with the man except for a few minutes when the painter was sent out to buy cigarettes. Since then I have often thought that this was an excuse to get the painter out of the room so that the man could talk frankly to us. It was the only opportunity we had to talk quite frankly. And we did.

I remember pointing out to this fellow that there was very little difference between what he had been telling us and what the IRA were saying to us. They were all concerned with poverty and deprivation. 'You know, the people in the South are saying exactly the same things as you are,' I told him. 'Do you see any useful purpose in the two parties meeting?' He said he didn't. It was obvious he would have been afraid to suggest such a meeting to his Loyalist cohorts. We asked if he would like us to keep in touch with him. He said he would.

We were all set to keep in touch with him, but three or four weeks later he was shot dead in his car. So that contact was abruptly ended too.

★ ★ ★

In the early 1980s I was invited to Derry for a weekend to stay with Will Warren. He was an English Quaker who had a great concern to make some kind of contribution towards peace and reconciliation. He came to the North on his own initiative and got to know all sorts of people while he lived in Derry. He was a gentle, quiet man who had a good approach with other people: he would never get their backs up.

He invited me to go and spend a night or two with him so that I could meet some of the groups of people he had been meeting with in Derry. One afternoon he took me to Martin McGuinness's house. I can't remember what was said exactly.[3]

With a number of these contacts it wasn't necessarily what was said on a particular occasion that was important. The important thing was that you made the contact and that you could contact each other in the future if any occasion warranted it.

★ ★ ★

I always had an open mind during my meetings with terrorists. I'd never met people like that before who held those kinds of views. You imagine terrorists must be desperate people to do the kinds of things they do. But when you meet them you find that they are not like that at all. They are very reasonable: they are people of very strong conviction and dedication and they have goals in life that they were brought up to believe in.

They are deeply convinced of the rightness of what they are doing which makes it all the harder to get through to them. If they were just terrorists, you'd feel it might be easier to get through to them in some ways. But they're not just terrorists – they're people just like the rest of us, although they happen to hold different views.

I remember the night Joe Cahill came to my house: in the course of chat he told me he had a cottage in a lovely quiet spot in the Wicklow mountains. He said how beautiful it was and how he loved to walk in the countryside and absorb its quietness and peacefulness. Those views sounded so strange coming from someone like him.

In meeting them, I think you have to accept that they are people like us and that they are entitled to their views as we are to ours. You don't approach these people aggressively, of course – they're used to that and they know how to deal with it. My role with them was largely a listening one – hearing what it was that they wanted. I do remember, though, discussing my views on violence with Daithí Ó Conaill and Seán MacStiofáin.[4]

* * *

Following the initial meeting in Eustace Street Meeting House I decided to call another meeting to which I invited a smaller number of people from both sides of the border. I arranged for the meeting to be held in Ballymascanlon Hotel near Dundalk. Again, the purpose of the meeting was purely for people to express their feelings about what was happening. And, again, no attempt was made to reach an agreement or a decision or anything like that. That would have been premature.

I chaired the meeting in a loose kind of way, leaving the floor open for people to speak. I remember the first person to speak was a man from the North and he fairly laid into the South and criticised the Republic for everything.

I was terribly pleased with the group of people from the South because none of them reacted at all. They just let him go on and on until he was exhausted. Other people then had the opportunity to contribute and the meeting continued with similar kinds of contributions, although they weren't all aggressive. It changed when the Northerners found that they weren't being attacked, but that they were being listened to.

The last person to speak at the meeting was the man who had spoken first and who had been so aggressive. He apologised for speaking the way he had and said he was pleased with how the meeting had gone. I felt that this was a great advance and that that was precisely what the meetings were about – trying to remove the divisions that arise out of misunderstandings.

We arranged more meetings at Ballymascanlon and I gradually built up a team of people from the South who were helpful in the discussions. For two or three years we held these meetings regularly during the summer months; we never held them in winter when travelling conditions might have been difficult. The meetings all followed the same pattern. They were all about listening to others and, I must say, I learnt an awful lot about the outlook of some Northerners. I think a lot of other people did too. I remember on one occasion a Jesuit from Dublin rang me up and said he had a party of Catholic students who had never spoken to a Protestant, but would like to. He asked if I could arrange it. It was just before one of the Ballymascanlon meetings, so I invited them to come to the meeting. And it went very well.

Following on from that, the students received an invitation to visit the North from some of the people they had met at the meeting. And the thing snowballed in exactly the way I hoped it would.

We met for a few years like that, just listening and learning. It was quite informal and I changed the personnel of the group over time so that more and more people became involved. One of the last meetings we had was with one of the Orange Lodges. Some people from the South told me they would like to meet some Orangemen. I wrote to Rev. Martin Smith to see if he could arrange for a group to meet us. He was away at the time, but his wife put us in touch with some Orangemen who said they would like to meet us. They said they would not come to Ballymascanlon, however, because it was too near the border.

We held the meeting, instead, in a Quaker meeting house north of the border. It was a very good meeting. We started off by asking them to tell us the history of the Orange Lodge and what they were trying to do. They started at the Book of Genesis and told us the history of the Orange Lodge from the Book of Genesis. This surprised me, but it was very interesting because it showed how their membership of the Orange Lodge is tied in with their religion and that its roots go very deep.

After several years I felt that the Ballymascanlon exercise had fulfilled what it was meant to do and that the time had come for it to be discontinued or it would go stale. By that time a lot of other initiatives were under way and, looking back, I think it was the right thing to do to drop it at that point.

* * *

I think every contact that was made north and south of the border for the purpose of creating understanding and seeing another person's point of view, thereby leading to reconciliation, was important. No matter how little or big it was.

Like everybody else, I learned a lot at Ballymascanlon that changed my understanding of the situation. My own feelings about the North changed over time as a result of meeting people with other viewpoints. I understand the Unionist point of view far more now than I used to. You nearly have to go and live there to understand the North. It's very easy down here to have preconceived ideas about people in the North, just as it is for them to have ideas about us.

One thing that struck me a number of times was that if they knew you were from the South – which they usually did as soon as you opened your mouth – they tended to be on the defensive before you had even said anything. They automatically expected that you were going to argue with them because you were from the South. I can understand that point of view now, whereas before that would have irritated me.

The more I learnt about the situation, the more complex I found it, but I never became despairing about it. I am still optimistic because there's great goodwill there. Northerners are very hospitable and I feel that every time I go to the North. I'm aware of the division, but behind it the people are very hospitable and welcoming. Once they find you are not there to criticise them, they will reach out the hand of friendship to you.

I never felt I had a solution to the situation. Definitely not! In fact, I never had strong feelings one way or another. I was interested from the point of view of people in our small island being divided rather than being united, but I never felt terribly strongly one way or another. If the North wanted to belong to the UK, that didn't bother me very greatly so long as it wasn't a festering sore, like it has been. I would feel the same about people in any part of the world where there is division that is festering and creating injustices and misunderstandings. I would always want to work towards reconciliation.

Any ceasefire, even for one day, is worthwhile. If it's years instead of days, then it's worth even more. One hopes that goodwill, having risen so far that so many people expressed their desire for peace and their longing for peace, surely cannot slip back again to things as they were. I hope the current ceasefires will continue and grow to fruition.

It would be a mistake to try and adopt a cut and dried solution; I never thought there was a cut and dried solution. It will always be a case of reconciliation leading towards a solution. Minds should be kept open and rigid decisions should not be taken because a solution will only work if people are ready to accept it.

In the past a certain number of people have always forced through their opinion, but that's not a solution. A solution can only be found when a way is found that is acceptable to all points of view. I think it is premature to try to decide what that solution should involve. I think minds should be kept open to allow thinking to develop and, where necessary, to re-adjust along the way. One of the fears of many people on both sides of the divide is that somehow a solution acceptable to some may be found and pushed through and that the door may then be closed to any satisfactory change after that.

Everybody has to accept that in the past Catholics were discriminated against and that they suffered greatly. That must not be lost sight of in trying to understand the Unionist point of view. But it does not mean that that is the only thing to be taken into account. Both sides have suffered and now we have got to find some way out instead of continuing to wallow.

I would not expect a common solution to be found within the next ten years, but we can be working towards one. Ten years is a very short time – it can go by so quickly – and I think time needs to be allowed to let things mellow for sufficient understanding of other people to take place.

Notes

1. Friends Service Council was a Quaker organisation concerned with overseas relief work.
2. Rachel recalls attending a couple of meetings with Daithí Ó Conaill in her father's office. She also remembers Daithíi and Victor meeting at her Dublin home on at least one occasion in the early 1980s.
3. Although there is no mention of any further contact with Martin McGuinness, Rachel remembers shaking Mr McGuinness's hand in Westmoreland Street café one time after he had met with Victor in his office.
4. Victor was a convinced pacifist. He would never have supported violence as a means of change in any circumstances, believing that all war and preparation for war was inconsistent with the teachings of Christ.

ELEVEN

AN EX-PRISONER COMES TO STAY

One day in the mid-1960s I received a letter addressed to me at Bewley's from a Scotsman called Jock who had a criminal record going back twenty-one years. He said he wanted to go straight, but that no one would help him. 'I don't blame them!' he wrote in brackets. He said he wanted to work and he wondered if I could help him. I wrote to him and asked him to come and see me in my office.

I watched the door with great interest when eleven o'clock came, on the appointed day, to see who came through it. I can still see him now. This shifty looking fellow marched in. He told me that he had come to Ireland to live with some relatives after his parents had died when he was young. He had joined the British Army when he turned sixteen, but after a while he and somebody else had broken into the canteen and stolen some cigarettes. He received a spell in jail for that. While he was in jail he got to know some other prisoners who lived by blowing the locks on safes. They taught him how to do this and so he became involved. That's how he got a further prison record.

I felt it was good that he wanted to work and I asked Alfred if there would be work for him on the farm at Ballyowen. He agreed – Alfred was great because he backed me up on a number of different projects – and it was decided that Jock would start work on a particular day.

He worked that day, but he didn't turn up the next. We thought that was the end of the matter and that we should have known it wouldn't work out. But a couple of days later I received a letter from him saying that he couldn't stick it because he was afraid other people would find out about him. He said he preferred to keep himself to himself because he was terrified people would find out about his prison record. So he said he couldn't work with the men at Ballyowen again.

We offered him work at Corrymeela. I wanted Connors cottage painted, anyway, and he agreed to do that. He came here every day and he got on great with the work. Before he had finished painting the cottage, he asked if he could come here to live. He said it would suit him because he would be anonymous here: there was no one to ask him where he came from. So he came to live in Connors cottage which was empty at the time because the Travellers had moved on.

Jock was terrific – a great character. He was completely honest and we ended up giving him the key of the house.[1] At the start he didn't know anything about Quakers, but he wanted to find out about them and he read everything he could get his hands on.

I remember one Sunday we were in a hurry out to meeting for worship and we left all the breakfast dishes in the kitchen unwashed. When we came back from meeting they were all washed, dried and neatly stacked on the counter. I knew it must have been Jock who had done them because nobody else had the key to the house. I thanked him very much for doing them and said it was very kind of him. He just smiled and said, 'Well, that's the Quaker way'.

He lived on the farm for a number of years[2] and worked with the cows and the hens. One day, he received a letter from somebody he knew in England who owned a shop and could offer him a better job. So he went over to England and he used to write to us regularly. He wasn't happy there, but he never asked to come back because, although he enjoyed the work on the farm, he knew it wouldn't lead to anything.

Notes
1. Heather received a letter, following her father's death, from a friend who said she still had a penknife 'given to me by the Scotsman who'd had a very chequered career, but who found contentment, purpose and self-respect living at Corrymeela'.
2. I have vague memories from early childhood of meeting Jock. He was a gifted craftsman and he made a child-sized table and chairs, a lorry and a boat for us to play with when we visited our grandparents.

REFLECTIONS

TWELVE

FAITH, HOPE
AND LOVE

I have always been interested in religion. In my early days I accepted what I heard from my parents, particularly what my mother said to me. My father, on the other hand, did not tell me what to believe: he encouraged me to develop my own ideas and to think for myself which was good.

I never heard anybody doubt what was in the Bible until after I had gone to Bootham. It was quite a shock to me to meet people who didn't think the gospels were relevant to today and who doubted that they were even true. At one stage, when I was about 16, I began to doubt what I had believed earlier. I was caught up in a conflict of what was true and what wasn't. I decided to throw everything overboard and not to believe anything because I wanted to see what I could come up with myself.

It was a time of searching and turmoil and I remember feeling very discontented when I returned to Dublin after leaving school because I felt confined at Churchtown Meeting.[1] I wanted to hear a wider range of views and I particularly wanted to hear about what was meaningful in the lives of other people. What motivated them? What made them tick? What was relevant to their lives?

I remember one day asking my mother if we could go to Eustace Street Meeting. I knew nothing about it except that it was a much larger meeting. 'Can't we go to Eustace Street because Churchtown is mouldy?' I said to her. 'Our meeting is so small that when somebody gets up to speak we always know what they're going to say before they even open their mouths.'

It surprised me, a few years later, when Churchtown did begin to show signs of new life. It grew larger and, with different people coming, you didn't know what they were going to say when they stood up to speak.[2] I changed my mind then about Churchtown: I became very happy there and I have been ever since. Recently we have had quite an influx of people who are sincerely seeking and who want the freedom to seek and to hear new ideas, just as I did. There are also a lot of children now and there is a flourishing Sunday School.

When I left school there was a very active Young Friends Group which met every Monday evening in Eustace Street Meeting House. We used to invite all sorts of people to come and talk to us and I was always very interested to hear what different people had to say. It did not matter who they were – I was always interested to hear about what was important to them and what was meaningful in their lives.

I have always loved to come across new ideas by talking to people and by reading books. It's a process that goes on for life. I can't remember who said, 'You start out on a search and you come back to the place you started from and see it as though for the first time.'

I remember feeling disappointed for a long time because I felt I had no religious experience. This wasn't correct because I was having it without knowing it. Some people, particularly those from Northern Ireland, could say that at a particular time on a particular date they had seen the light. It seemed so cut and dry and I wanted that: I wanted an experience that would transform me. Looking back now I see that I was looking for an experience that would get rid of all my problems. I had yet to realise that it is in facing problems and coming through them that one finds the experience.

I remember one Saturday night while I was getting ready for bed I thought of the words, 'God is love'. I saw those words in a way I had never seen them before: I saw that God's love working in someone's life was a positive force and that this is what Jesus' message was all about. I had known those words since I was old enough to know anything out of the Bible, but I had never seen them in that same light. Next morning I stood up during meeting for worship and simply repeated those words, 'God is love', and sat down again. A short time later an elderly Friend stood up and seemed to query whether or not God was love. This nearly paralysed me. He didn't mean it in an unhelpful way: I realised later that he had, in fact, been agreeing with me. It was just the way he had put it. My experience has developed a lot since then, but it's all been a fulfilment of those words that I knew right from the start. The experience has grown and has become part of my life.

If I was asked to put religious experience into simple words, which is not easy to do, I would say that I believe there is a power greater than ourselves and outside of ourselves that can touch us, mould us, guide us, strengthen us and shed light on life's path. That power is love. To know this power is not a matter of intellectual understanding, but a matter of experience. To orientate our lives towards the spirit of love is the way to the experience. If we aim to do this, it profoundly affects our values and our whole list of priorities: it affects our attitudes to our fellow men and our attitudes to material possessions. I don't see any division between that and the way an evangelical expresses his or her beliefs although we are using different words. It is the same spirit that we are talking about – 'He that liveth in love liveth in God.' I think people who really experience this find that they not only want to bring their own lives into harmony with the spirit of love, but that they also want to create conditions around them that are in harmony with that spirit.

I remember one time at a meeting on management in industry a man introduced the discussion by saying that we create conditions around us in accordance with our sense of values. I think that's true. If we are touched by the spirit that is in us then we will want to create conditions around us that are in harmony with it.

People have asked me again and again whether the changes I made in Bewley's Cafes were in any way to do with my religion. It is a very hard question to answer, but I think the simple answer is, 'Yes'. The formation of the Bewley Community was an expression of the spirit working in my own life. I think it is paramount to accept that there is a spirit of love that can work in us and to try and live in harmony with that spirit. It is a matter of fact that the spirit exists and that it can profoundly affect us and what we do.

I remember one time Dundalk County Council was being very negligent in its provision for Travellers. They were very hard nuts to crack and on one occasion a special meeting was organised to consider the provision for Travellers and I was invited to attend. There was one man in particular who stood out because he was blocking every single proposal. 'I came here tonight with my mind made up and I am not going to change it,' he said. He was dead against the idea of anything being provided for Travellers and we made no progress at the meeting.

Some years later I heard that Dundalk had got the go ahead for some plans and I asked how on earth had they managed to get past this particular man. I was told that the man had a brother who was a missionary and that when he was home on holidays he had heard about his brother holding up provision for Travellers. He spoke to him about it and pointed out the wrongfulness of his position. The man ended up changing his line and supporting the proposals.

That's just one illustration of how the spirit in a person can change his surroundings. There is no division in the spirit of Christ: it's just that different people use different words to describe it.

* * *

I have always had a great belief in prayer. It has always been important to me and it has definitely become more important over the years. Sometimes we ask for a problem or a difficulty to be removed, but that isn't always God's way. What we need to do is ask for wisdom to see the right solution, to follow the right way and to ask for the strength to do that.

I was once asked by a journalist if I could draw a picture of God. Straightaway I said, 'No'. I explained that I would not want to even try because if I could draw a picture of God that would limit him to my imagination and understanding. And that kind of God would be of no use to me.

The fact that Quakers believe we are all equal in God's eyes does not mean that we are all the same, thank goodness. Life would be very dull if that were the case. I believe that within each of us there is something that reaches out to something greater than ourselves. Just like a flower bud turns to light and warmth to unfold and blossom, we reach out to something to help us grow to our full potential. I think that is the purpose of life.

I pray daily – many times daily – and I don't think I ever miss a day. But my prayers are not confined to special times. I pray while I am doing other things: I could be digging the garden or something like that.

I think the best way for me to illustrate my belief in prayer is by using the image of the television. There are waves in the air all around us that we are totally unaware of unless we stop to think about them. We have to turn on the television for us to be brought consciously into touch with this whole world of waves around us. By pressing a knob we see pictures and we hear people speaking that we wouldn't be aware of unless we made this connection. And that is the way I think it is with spiritual things.

The power of love is always there and it can have a profound effect on our lives and on situations, but we have to do our part by being aware of it and making a connection with it. Just as we can't see the connection between the sun and us, we can feel the effect of its heat on us. So I think it is with prayer.

Prayer is not so much about asking God for things: when we're small we tend to think it is about asking God to do this, that and the other. I think it's more about being aware of the spirit of God that is around us and seeing how his spirit would lead us, seeing what in our lives is in accordance or harmony with the spirit and seeing what is out of harmony with it.

Prayer brings us into harmony with the spirit of God. It is about making ourselves available to his spirit of love. I pray for bigger problems too, like famine and poverty. It is harder to see how that works though.

A couple of years ago I dreamt that I was in Churchtown Meeting one Sunday morning and that I felt a tremendous sense of well-being and of being surrounded by light and love. I just relaxed, as one might relax in the sunshine, and later in the dream this aura of warmth and light and love seemed to reach out to other situations and to other people. This dream occurred at a time that I had been most conscious of praying for other people and other situations. I don't understand for a minute how it works, but I believe there is a power of love and I'm quite happy to use that power in the belief that it does help.

★ ★ ★

Quaker meetings for worship are about being aware of the presence of God. Not about coming into the presence of God – because we are always in his presence – but about being aware of it. I think we can be aware of it at different levels of consciousness. Finding our way through the path of life with all its ups and downs and the problems that we meet along the way, it is very easy to forget the power of prayer and to wallow in our own difficulties instead, thereby making our difficulties worse. I have always loved the verse, 'Be still and know that I am God' (Psalm 46:10). That stillness is very important because when we sit down quietly we realise how much we're running around inside, as it were. As we become aware of this and think quietly and just open our minds to what the spirit is saying to us, we can feel something inside us relaxing. I think we can go on relaxing like that on several layers: it is something that comes out of the quietness. This reaffirms our belief in God as we open ourselves again to the presence of the spirit and its power to influence us.

This kind of stillness is a tremendous help in life as we face its ups and downs and gain fresh inspiration. And while we can, of course, do this on our own, I think there is something special to be gained from doing it with others in meeting for worship.

There's a healing group that meets together in Churchtown Meeting House once a month and we pray for anyone we feel needs prayer. We've all felt from time to time that we reach a deeper level of worship in our little group than in the larger group that meets together on a Sunday morning. That's not in any way to cry down the Sunday morning worship, but maybe when you get a small group of people meeting together with a special purpose there's a special power there.

More and more a word I have come to like is 'wholeness'. I think physical illness is often a symptom of some deeper need and that it's more important to pray for the deeper need than it is to pray for the symptom.

When we pray for people who have difficulties of one sort or another or for people with health problems, I think it is important to see them as we believe God would want them to be – whole people. We should not dwell on their illnesses or their problems so much as on the power of God to help them and to heal them.

I think there's a great searching today and a great hunger for spirituality that has meaning and power. There's been a great dropping away from organised religion which too often has become a mumbo-jumbo of repetitions and thinking along lines that are not always alive and filled with meaning for us. I think it is better to be still and quiet in order to see what is coming to us from the spirit.

* * *

I am not really afraid of death. At times when I've been down I have had some reservations about it, but I wouldn't say I am ordinarily afraid of it. I remember the first time I really thought about death was once when I was talking to a Christian Brother. He worked with deaf people and we used to employ some deaf men at Danum.[3] He was eighty-four the last time I went to visit him and he wasn't well. He knew that his time was nearly up and he said to me, 'I'm afraid to die, you know.'

I was surprised because, being a Christian Brother, I thought that he wouldn't have minded. That was the first time I thought about being afraid of dying. I felt I wasn't afraid, thank goodness: at that time my own death seemed so far away it didn't seem anything to worry about.

I don't worry much about life after death because I'm quite happy to leave it until I get there. Except for very short periods in my life I have always believed in a life after death because I can't see that this life makes any sense if there isn't something following on. I see life after death as a continuation of spiritual growth. As regards what form that takes and whether we know each other and all those sorts of questions, I just let them come through my mind and go out again. I have no particular theory and I don't think it is necessary to have a particular theory on it. It takes us all our time and energy to live our lives in this world. I think it makes sense to leave the next life until we get there.

Notes
1. Churchtown Quaker Meeting. For further information on Quakers see Appendix.
2. By 1941 the membership of Churchtown Quaker Meeting had grown to 112.
3. Winifred remembers, as a young child, peeping into the living room on one occasion when one of these deaf men was holding his wedding reception. She remembers being aware of a 'weird' atmosphere: even though the room was full of people, hardly anyone was speaking.

THIRTEEN

'LOVE THY NEIGHBOUR AS THYSELF'

Some people feel that religion has had its day and that it is now remote from our everyday lives. But I believe it should be an intimate part of our lives. When Jesus was asked which was the greatest commandment, he answered, 'Thou shalt love the Lord thy God'. Some people find this difficult. How can we love God whom we have not seen? We remember that even one of the disciples said to Jesus, 'Show us the Father and we shall be satisfied'. He answered, 'He that hath seen me hath seen the Father'. He did not mean his physical appearance, but the spirit which he showed us – the spirit that inspired all his words and actions.

To the Samaritan woman he said, 'God is spirit and they that worship Him must worship Him in spirit and in truth'. And to Nicodemus he said, 'The wind blows where it wills, you hear the sound of it but cannot tell from where it comes or to where it goes; so is everyone that is born of the spirit'.

We know the spirit of God as the spirit of love working in people's lives. We cannot say how it comes or goes, but we feel the warmth of it when it is there making life creative and worthwhile. We can see it in others and we can know it in ourselves, moving us to be better people than we might otherwise have been.

We can resist this spirit or we can respond to it by orientating our lives to it, by pausing in our busy routine and letting it take hold of us, showing us how far we have strayed from it and acted contrary to it. It can bring us back again by our being willing to let go of that in ourselves which is inconsistent with it and being ready to follow the actions which it prompts us to do. In this way it can become a positive force in our lives.

'Thou shalt love the Lord thy God'. This then is the most important thing. It can be a daily experience for each of us.

After he gave us the greatest commandment, Jesus then added, 'A second like unto it, thou shalt love thy neighbour as thyself'. We cannot separate these two, they are part of the same experience. You cannot really do one without the other. This must begin with those we mix with day by day. Have we feelings of goodwill towards them? Are we considerate and understanding, patient and sensitive to their feelings and to their needs?

We see a starving child on our television screens. We are deeply moved. Yes, this is our brother, our sister. We must help. We do help and we are right to do so. But our help has cost us little, really. We have given what we can afford. The child and his family have made no real impact on our lives. Suppose the child and his family came to live next door to us. How would we feel about them then?

Perhaps a Travelling family is camped near our home. The children are sleeping on straw on the ground in this harsh wintry weather. There are many more like them. Yes, in many cases the camping sites are untidy and dirty and the children are a nuisance with their begging: they have been taught to do this since they were old enough to do it.

Can we see here our neighbour? And can we love him or her as ourselves? 'If only they could change some of their ways that are so objectionable,' we say. Perhaps they would if we could change some of ours: our hardness of heart, our stubborn refusal to give them the chance of a way of life that would allow them to change. Also, our inability to see them and to know them as people like ourselves.

To do this we might change their lives. It might change our lives too, and a new richness and warmth of fellowship might flow through it. The love of God might become a greater reality to us, as well as to them.

* * *

There is in each of us the capacity to respond to the power of love, though often it is hidden below many things. Fear, unhappiness, bitterness, destroying our faith in our fellowmen and in ourselves, yet none the less it is there, an urge towards something higher, something better, like a flower turning its head towards the sun. We must allow it to find expression in ourselves.

I remember a friend of mine saying to me on one occasion: 'I can feel myself changing; I am becoming a Christian.' His actions showed the reality and depth of his experience. He had become aware of the power of love and had responded to it. He was able to make the response, but some people may need our help and understanding over a long period of time. We must never lose hope.

I remember a man whose early life had been thwarted by unhappiness, leaving him an embittered anti-social adult. He followed his destructive path for many years, but never lost the desire for a better way. He asked me if I could help him. I tried, but no progress seemed to be made and I wondered if it would ever be made. He seemed to know my thoughts because he wrote to me saying, 'Don't lose faith in me. If you lose faith in me, I am lost'. I felt reproved for my doubts. Some time later he came to realise that other people really did care about him and something in him responded to this. It grew and blossomed in his life and gradually the bitterness that had dominated him in previous years gave way to the greater power of love. He became a different man, living a useful, constructive life, doing many kindly acts for others.

When we meet people who are difficult and anti-social, we should pause to wonder what has made them so. What stands between them and the happiness they seek?

* * *

Jesus tells us that if we are bringing our gift to the altar and remember that our brother has something against us, we should leave our gift and go home, be reconciled with our brother first and then go back and offer our gift. Goodwill towards our fellowmen is part of the true spirit of worship.

A friend of mine remarked to me recently that if we harbour grievances against others, there can be no growth of spirit in such circumstances. We injure ourselves as well as injuring others. We harden something that is sensitive within us. It becomes easier to be careless again, even to hurt others who were not involved in the original incident. It is like an illness that eats into our soul and may deeply affect our whole outlook on life, and our health also.

We know only too well how much trouble in the world arises from ill-feeling harboured between individuals. It can poison our personal life and it can warp our community life, our national and international life. It all begins with personal relationships. If we are to follow the way of love we must learn to understand others better, and so be able to forgive, to restore a relationship which has become embittered to one of goodwill.

When we become aware that we have upset others, do we try to make amends? We do well to pause quietly from time to time to dwell on this, to be willing to let it happen.

Jesus taught us to pray that we should be forgiven our shortcomings as we forgive those of others. In forgiving others, in bringing reconciliation, we ourselves become reconciled with the spirit of love and we are freed from the bitterness, the resentment and the hardness of heart that was hindering us.

Can we cherish an understanding and forgiving spirit?

★ ★ ★

If we try to follow the spirit we cannot put first our own welfare and that of our particular group, but we will work for the good of all men. We will seek a way of life that gives this concrete expression and is consistent with our belief that all men are brothers. We must be ready to play our part in changing all that is contrary to this, working to remove injustice and oppression wherever we may find it. Too often we are too slow in this. Wrongs are ignored and conflicts are left unresolved until they grow in proportion and we are involved in a strike or a war. We then have to concentrate on trying to bring this to an end whereas, had we been alert and been active at an earlier stage, we would have tackled the matter at a time when it would have been easier to find a solution. In this way, much unnecessary suffering and ill-feeling would have been avoided.

We have only to read the papers, listen to the radio and watch the television to know of the troubles in the world, of the atrocious things which man can do to man. That is one side of the picture. The other side is the tremendous goodwill which is in most people. Often we only find this out when we are in trouble or there is a crisis of some sort: then we are touched and cheered by the kindness and goodwill which are shown. Do we give enough expression to this normally? Can we not make it more vocal, turn it into more positive action to make the world a happier place for us all? Do we just dream idly about these thoughts or do we do what we can to join with others in strengthening and promoting all that is for good in the world? Do we try to live continually in that spirit which seeks to remove the causes of conflict and injustice and to promote the good of all men?

★ ★ ★

How much of our troubles in life are caused by fear?

In 1960 my wife and I were visiting Kenya. It was just at the end of the Mau Mau emergency and I remember one of our European hostesses saying that it was necessary to protect the windows at night and to have a good watchdog, as one could not trust the Africans. She was a pleasant, kindly person, but her fear was real.

We visited another European family living at a social centre in the African part of the town. On arrival we saw African children playing outside with one white child among them. At an open door we found our friend.[1] During our visit various Africans came and went and obviously felt that here they would have a friendly reception.

The building was a bungalow, the windows were unprotected at night and there was no watchdog. An African neighbour remarked, 'People often wonder why your friends are not afraid to live here unprotected; it makes them think.'

What was it in the way of life, the attitude and the actions of the first family that had led to conditions where there was a state of fear and the need for protection whereas those of the second family had led to conditions where fear had not made protection necessary? In the First Epistle of John we read that perfect love casts out fear. Here we could see the truth of this in action.

What kind of lives are we living? What sort of conditions are we building up for ourselves and the next generation? Are we building up conditions leading to hatred and fear, or to trust and goodwill?

'Thou shalt love the Lord thy God' and 'Thou shalt love thy neighbour as thyself'. This is an experience to be lived in every situation in which we find ourselves.

Notes
1.   This friend was Walter Martin, the English Quaker who accompanied Victor to some of his meetings with Republicans and Loyalists.

FOURTEEN

UNDILUTED HELL

Although I have no real regrets looking back, I'd hate to live my life again. Parts of it were undiluted hell and, at times, I thought I'd never come through it.

Looking back you see life as a whole and there was no part of my life, even the hell parts, that didn't make a positive contribution eventually. I think if you've never suffered, then there's a whole area of life that is closed to you. What is important in life is not so much what happens to us, but how we react to what happens.

My problems were not simply the result of shyness. I'm sure my shyness problem didn't help, but it was much more than that.

Nobody likes to admit that they might be a bit cracked: it's much easier to say that you're very shy and that you want to know how to overcome that than to say that you think you're slipping in the top storey. But that is exactly how I felt at a time in the 1940s when I was undergoing psychoanalysis.

* * *

I had made friends with a man called Basil Rákóczi who had come to live in Dublin in 1939. He was an artist, but he was also a lay psychoanalyst.[1] He was a very nice fellow and he was very interesting. He was living in Paris, but he came to live in Ireland during the war years and he warned me that he would return to France once the war was over.[2] As a result of hearing him talk about psychoanalysis I felt I would like to dig deeper to understand myself more and to help my life to flow more freely. I ended up going to him for analysis on and off for several years.

In psychoanalysis you just lie down on a couch and relax and say whatever comes into your head, without censoring it. The point is to bring out the rubbish that you've collected up over the years. It's all about loosening up emotions and memories from the past, bringing them to the surface to get rid of the ones that are causing you trouble. It sounds very simple, but it takes a while to get used to.

It is a very disturbing process – you're constantly digging up things from the past – and it can vitally affect your relationships with other people at the time. Others might not notice it beyond thinking that you're being very bad-tempered on a particular day and that kind of thing. They don't realise what is behind your behaviour and they don't feel half as upset about it as you do. At the time I was undergoing psychoanalysis I was already married with children. The analysis made me super touchy and this caused friction and tension both inside the family and outside of it.

Business weighed heavily on top of that too: there were extra pressures in the firm during the war years. The psychoanalysis affected my whole life really. Several times during the analysis I came to the point where I said to Basil that I thought I must have had a tremendous wish not to be born because I often had an apprehension of new situations. For instance, if I went on a train journey I'd settle into my corner of the carriage and read or look out the window. I would just do whatever it was I wanted to do and then I'd be sorry when I reached my destination because I wouldn't want to get out. I'd rather have stayed in my little cocoon. That's a trivial thing, but it illustrates the point.

'Why don't you ask your mother if there was anything about your birth that was difficult and which might explain this feeling?' Basil said to me one day. When I asked my mother she was amazed that I suspected there had been anything difficult about my birth because she had never told me and, of course, I couldn't possibly have remembered. She told me she had been three days in labour with me and that the doctors had had to use instruments to get me out. They'd poked around inside her with various instruments and when I was finally born I was facially damaged. She said my face had been just like a ball of pulp and that she thought I would be terribly disfigured when I grew up.

★ ★ ★

Looking back on it, I think psychoanalysis was a very valuable experience for me. I don't recommend it as being a cure-all for everybody: I think lots of people would find it too disturbing and an unsuitable way for them. However, I think I eventually gained a lot of understanding about myself. It also helped me to understand other people and I'm very grateful I had the experience. In the end it helped me to become calmer in facing life.

Notes

1. Basil Rákóczi spent his childhood between England and France. His father was Hungarian while his mother hailed from Cork. In 1935 he set up the Society for Creative Psychology in London which attracted painters who drew on experiences in psychological techniques. In the 1940s he became involved with The White Stag Group of avant garde painters in Dublin. Rákóczi shared Victor's pacifist views and he reportedly met Ghandi while travelling in India in the 1930s. During his time in Ireland he became a member of the Religious Society of Friends. His paintings have been exhibited a number of times in Dublin, the last occasion being a retrospective exhibition held in the Gorry Gallery, Molesworth Street in 1996.

2. He left Dublin in 1946.

FIFTEEN

RETIREMENT

When I retired from the firm in 1977 I was very glad to have more time to devote to Travellers and to enjoy being in the open air on the farm. Until the end of 1988 I went into my office in town several days a week to continue my work with Travellers.

I have very much enjoyed my retirement years, but I mourn the fact that time is passing so quickly. Farm work keeps me busy and now I wonder how I ever found time to run a business.

It is an interesting time to be alive and I am thankful that I have plenty of interests to occupy my time. I love being outdoors and I find relaxation through beauty in its various forms – nature, music and art. I seem to find little time to read; when I do, it is usually about other people and their experiences.

I tend now to take the days as they come. I don't look to the future and I don't make plans – I just do whatever seems appropriate on the day. I have always been an optimist and I still am an optimist.

★ ★ ★

I don't go into the cafes anymore. Other people sometimes tell me that Bewley's is a different place now, but I don't know.

Winnie and I make a weekly shopping trip to the Dublin suburbs, but we rarely venture into the city centre: we dislike traffic and we see no need to go into town.

We buy Bewley's tea and coffee from the Blackrock shop and we believe the quality of the beverages has been maintained. We only occasionally buy food from Bewley's because we are self-sufficient as far as possible, eating our own produce. We have cattle, hens, geese and

ducks on the farm. We also grow our own fruit and vegetables –
potatoes, carrots, onions, celery, peas, broad beans, turnips, gooseberries,
rhubarb, blackcurrants, apples, raspberries and plums.

★ ★ ★

As a youngster, I thought that when you were thirty that was it, you'd
really had it. And when I got to thirty myself I shoved it on to forty. And
it's gradually gone up over the years. I used to think that at eighty I would
be rather doddery. And I wondered if I would still be able to milk a cow.
Now I wonder the same about when I'm ninety!

AFTERWORD

My grandfather did not, as he had wondered, go on to milk cows at the age of ninety. This despite his optimism and good health at the time I interviewed him. Old age crept up on him, as it does with everybody, with its inevitable physical and mental decline. Even after he was diagnosed with Parkinson's disease, however, he was determined to look after himself and to remain on the farm he loved so well.

The time did eventually come when he saw the wisdom in moving some place where he would receive twenty-four-hour care. And so in 1998 he moved to New Lodge, a Quaker nursing home in Donnybrook. He brought a few belongings with him to make his room more homely. One of these treasured items was the brightly-coloured bedspread that had been a gift from a group of Travellers many years before. Of course, he missed his beloved farm and the familiar views of the Dublin mountains. The well-kept gardens at the nursing home were simply not the same.

He spent some long and lonely nights in New Lodge as he tried to come to terms with physical, emotional and spiritual changes. He also had a number of vivid dreams, which he shared with his three daughters. My mother felt that, by doing this, he was trying to indicate to them how he was feeling, as well as preparing them for what he hoped was imminent.

On several occasions he dreamt that he was climbing a mountain (in his youth he had enjoyed hill walking). The ascent became easier with each dream and he told Winifred that, by climbing the mountain, he felt he was leaving behind his cares and responsibilities. She noticed that, at about this time, her father seemed to achieve a new level of peace and acceptance, and that, as time went on, the sense of peace became more pronounced.

About six months later Victor dreamt that he was in a small boat on Clifden Bay (in his younger days he used to go fishing there in his rowing boat). He dreamt that he tried to get out of the boat, but that it kept moving around; he realised he was in his pyjamas and he grew afraid of catching pneumonia. After a while, however, he became aware of a warm glow welling up inside and spreading throughout his body, keeping him warm. He said that he found this dream helpful and reassuring.

On Wednesday 19th May 1999, three weeks after he had this dream and just five days short of his eighty-seventh birthday, Victor Bewley died peacefully.

★ ★ ★

It cannot have been a surprise to anyone that Victor was altruistic in his death, just as he had been during his lifetime: he donated his body to Trinity College Dublin for the purpose of medical research. It was to be over a year before his remains could finally be laid to rest. A memorial meeting, however, was held in Churchtown Quaker Meeting House three days after he died. The room was packed not only with members of the Bewley clan and of The Religious Society of Friends, but also with former Bewley's staff and Travellers as well as a well-known trade union leader and a representative of President Mary McAleese.

During the meeting my mother said, 'On Wednesday morning a very special light went out, on Thursday morning a little girl in England went to her church and lit a candle for her great-grandad and, in a few weeks time, a new little person will join our extended family. Death is not the end, but part of the cycle of life.'

She went on to read the following verses penned by the Quaker hymnist, John Greenleaf Whittier, which she had shared with my grandfather the night before he died. It was a hymn that he himself had often quoted:

> *Drop thy still dews of quietness,*
> *Till all our strivings cease;*
> *Take from our souls the strain and stress,*
> *And let our ordered lives confess*
> *The beauty of thy peace.*

Breathe through the heats of our desire
Thy coolness and thy balm;
Let sense be dumb, let flesh retire;
Speak through the earthquake, wind and fire,
O still small voice of calm!

Following Victor's death The Parish of the Travelling People held a Mass of Thanksgiving for him. The mass was celebrated by his old friend and colleague, Bishop Christy Jones, who had succeeded Victor in the post of government adviser on the settlement of Travellers. It was a moving and meaningful service.

Another long-time friend and co-worker, Monsignor Thomas Fehily, wrote an appreciation, which appeared in *The Travelling Times* magazine. 'Victor Bewley had a deep Christian love and concern for every person, but he had a special kind of care for anyone in need or who lived in any kind of rejection,' he wrote.

'Victor's love for Travellers was not just a love he felt, but it showed itself in good and courageous work for them. For over thirty years he gave hundreds of lectures all over Ireland about their suffering. And this was not always easy. In most places he was met by opposition; in some by bitterness and rejection. But he never lost his quiet calm and patience and he never criticised or judged those who opposed him.

'Now that there are some improvements in the lives of Travellers, it is easy to forget the dedication and courage of this great friend of Travellers. Trinity College honoured him with an honorary degree, but he would much prefer to be remembered in the hearts of Travellers.'

Throughout his life Victor was far more concerned with giving than receiving and I can remember only one occasion when he asked me for something. It was during one of my last visits to see him in the nursing home. His request was simple and, to be honest, I think it was for my benefit as much as his: he wanted me to share a blessing with him.

I prayed a traditional Celtic blessing that had always reminded me of him because he always seemed happiest when he was close to nature. And I suspected that it was in the great outdoors – whether on his farm or in Connemara – that he often felt closest to God.

The blessing I shared with him in the nursing home that day was the same one I prayed on the occasion of the interment of his remains on 11th July 2000 at Temple Hill – the Quaker burial ground at Blackrock, Co Dublin.

Deep peace of the running wave to you,
Deep peace of the flowing air to you,
Deep peace of the quiet earth to you,
Deep peace of the shining stars to you,
Deep peace of the Son of Peace to you.

I am quite sure that anyone who had the privilege of meeting Victor Bewley found him to be a man of peace – a peacemaker as well as a man who loved peace. It is only right, therefore, that he should be at deep peace now.

APPENDIX

Quakers

The Religious Society of Friends (Quakers) was founded in 1652 by an Englishman, George Fox. An earnest young man with a detailed knowledge of the Bible, he believed Christ spoke directly to those who sought him. He and his fellow-seekers called themselves Children of Light and then Friends of Truth, which in due course became The Religious Society of Friends. The term Quaker is a nickname dating from the early days.

Friends believe that God exists in everyone and that every human being has the potential to communicate with God and to experience divine love and guidance. They believe that loving God and other people gives meaning and purpose to life. Their conviction that God's light is in everyone is based on the life and teachings of Jesus Christ. Following His example, they try to understand people of all classes, colours and creeds. They have always put men and women on an equal footing.

The Religious Society of Friends has no paid ministers and all members are encouraged to serve the society in accordance with their gifts and abilities. Business meetings are conducted in a prayerful manner.

Quakers are not puritanical, but aim for simplicity and integrity. They enjoy material blessings, but try to resist materialistic attitudes, believing that earthly possessions are held in trust.

They have no creed because they believe that a written statement can limit the interpretation of God. Friends find that, whereas words and arguments may cause division, the shared experience of seeking to put Christ's message into practice can bring them closer together.

Meetings for Worship do not follow a formal programme. Instead, Quakers gather in silence believing that God will lead them to 'worship Him in spirit and in truth' as Jesus taught. They believe everyone can share inwardly in offering love and worship to God. Anyone present may feel guided to speak about his or her own experience, to pray aloud or to read from the Bible or other spiritual writings.

Some people find the silence helpful in seeking guidance about personal problems or emotional or intellectual conflicts. Others become absorbed in an experience of worship that removes them from their daily concerns.

Friends aim to encourage the right use of natural resources. They work for racial harmony and oppose any use of torture or violence, believing that all war is inconsistent with the spirit and teaching of Christ.

The above information is compiled from several leaflets published by Dublin Monthly Meeting of the Religious Society of Friends.